W9-CHP-624

A Rainbow Book

The
Whipped
PARENT

*Hope for Parents
Raising an
Out-of-Control Teen*

KIMBERLY ABRAHAM, MSW, CSW
MARNEY STUDAKER-CORDNER, MSW, CSW
WITH KATHRYN O'DEA

Rainbow Books, Inc.
FLORIDA

Library of Congress Cataloging-in-Publication Data

Abraham, Kimberly, 1961-
  The whipped parent : hope for parents raising an out-of-control teen / by
Kimberly Abraham, Marney Studaker-Cordner, with Kathryn O'Dea.
      p. cm.
Includes bibliographical references and index.
  ISBN 1-56825-092-4 (trade pbk. : alk. paper)
1. Conduct disorders in adolescence—Popular works. 2. Oppositional defiant
disorder in adolescence—Popular works. 3. Parenting—Popular works. I.
Studaker-Cordner, Marney, 1969- II. O'Dea, Kathryn, 1942- III. Title.
  RJ506.C65A25 2003
  616.89'00835—dc21

                                                2003009698

The Whipped Parent
Hope for Parents Rasing an Out-of-Control Teen
Copyright © 2003
by Kimberly Abraham, MSW, CSW,
Marney Studaker-Cordner, MSW, CSW,
with Kathryn O'Dea

ISBN 978-1-56825-092-2

Published by
Rainbow Books, Inc.
P. O. Box 430
Highland City, FL 33846-0430

Editorial Offices and Wholesale/Distributor Orders
Telephone: (863) 648-4420
Email: RBIbooks@aol.com

Individualsí Orders
Toll-free Telephone (800) 431-1579
http://www.AllBookStores.com

Produced and Printed in the United States of America

Acknowledgments

Special thanks to Rodney Studaker, for his editorial work and for his poems, which helped begin and end the book.

We also want to acknowledge the court workers of Genesee and Lapeer counties, Michigan, in particular Lori Curtiss of Lapeer, for sharing thoughts and ideas about working with conduct disordered adolescents. We admire your dedication to the tremendous number of children and families you serve every day.

To Nancy Rodda, Paul Jordan and the CAS staff at Genesee County Community Mental Health. No agency compares to your expertise and heart in treating severely emotionally disturbed youth and families. We are proud to have had the opportunity to work alongside you.

To Janet Morin and the staff at the Comfort Inn of Davison, Michigan, for providing the friendly and comfortable atmosphere that allowed us to concentrate and write this book.

Thanks also to Thomas Pope and Carolyn Voight for their support and encouragement these last two years.

A special thanks to Bill Abraham, for teaching the value of taking the negative emotions out before reacting. This was a true lesson in personal growth.

To our husbands, Bob Hornacek and Mark Cordner, for their encouragement, support and patience during the many hours we spent writing. To our children, Jason, Nathan, Rayna, Kyle, Courtney, Kirstyn and Faith — we love you. And to our parents, for always believing in us and loving us unconditionally.

Special thanks to our publishers, Betty and Betsy, for all your hard work and support.

Most of all, thank you to the adolescents and their parents who have allowed us the pleasure and privilege of working with them. Your courage inspires us.

The Whipped Parent

by Rodney Studaker

I'm whipped, I'm beat, I'm dead on my feet,
My child is quite out of control.
I quit, I'm done, this isn't much fun,
I'm trapped and have nowhere to go.

My hopes, my dreams, to me it just seems
Are crushed by my kid every day.
He'll push, he'll shove, to the limits of love,
'Til I wish that he'd just go away.

I've screamed, I've cried, I have certainly tried,
But relief is nowhere in sight.
He lies, he swears, he just doesn't care —
I'm afraid I am losing the fight.

I want, I wish, for much more than this,
But anger just tears me apart.
I'll try anything, let's give it a fling
Point the way, I'm ready to start . . .

Contents

A Personal Introduction

I just swore at another talk show. You know the ones: the guests are rotten, nasty teenagers and their *whipped* parents. Kids who refuse to go to school and the parents who are hauled into court, fined and put in jail for their teens' choices. These parents are so desperate, they've resorted to going on a talk show in an effort to control their child. In return for their efforts, they will be picked apart and humiliated. Their teens will be ridiculed and condemned. No one will leave feeling better — except the audience and the host. The guests will leave feeling sick.

Society has stripped us — the parents — of our power, and we don't know where to turn. Many of us fear not only what our child might do next, but how *we* will be punished for their actions. What has happened in our country? How has it come to be that parents pay the price for the crimes of today's adolescents? In the land of *Little House on the Prairie*, Ma and Pa Ingalls wouldn't have worried. Their kids were practically angels. Mr. and Mrs. Olsen, on the other hand, are turning over in their graves. What if they had been called to the school every time Willie acted up? Nellie Olsen would have been sent to boot camp, where it's legal to physically and mentally abuse these kids. Extremes . . . that's what our society has come to. Where is the middle ground?

As a clinical therapist specializing in oppositional-defiant and conduct disordered adolescents, I have seen a drastic increase in children with extreme negative behaviors. *Oppositional-defiant disorder* and *conduct disorder* are labels or diagnoses that professionals use in the mental health field. Simply put, we're talking about kids who fight against society's norms and rules.

Oppositional-defiant kids are negative, defiant, disobedient and hostile toward authority figures. They lose their tempers, argue and refuse to comply with the requests of parents, teachers, therapists, even the local librarian. Any adult who tries to set a limit is fair game. This type of adolescent is often angry, resentful, spiteful and vindictive. They deliberately annoy people and blame others for their poor choices and negative behavior.

Conduct disordered kids are all of the above and then some. They engage in severely dangerous and illegal behaviors. They are often the school bullies, threatening peers and adults. They fight, carry weapons and do drugs. They lie, steal, set fires and deliberately destroy other people's property. They are often truant from school, stay out past curfew and run away from home, despite their parents' efforts to stop them. These teens consistently and seriously violate the rules and laws of society.

I'm not just a therapist dealing with these adolescents, I am also the parent of one of these kids. A kid whom I often felt was born just to piss me off. I was angry, scared, frustrated, hurt and defensive when approached by school officials, the police, neighbors, my family and friends. I was guilt-ridden and felt out of control.

My child was running — and ruining — my life. I tried to get help, but found none. I tried counseling and read every parenting book out there, only to come away more frustrated and guilt-ridden when nothing worked. I started developing my own approach — desperately trying to regain my emotional well-being.

Dealing with my own life led me to specialize in this population of kids as a therapist. My mission became to help other parents survive, and even find humor, while struggling to raise one of these kids. My son, whom I'll call *Jack* for fear he'll sue me, was my inspiration, *or maybe my desperation*, in writing this book.

It is my coauthors' and my hope that society will begin to find middle ground regarding today's youth. Until then, our mission is to balance the power. Parents have felt threatened by schools, courts and other systems for much too long. We don't care if you were a *good parent* or not while your child was young. There's no point in debating *why* your teen is out of control now. The point is, you need help handling today and tomorrow. Yesterday is gone.

This book was written to help you find the hope and humor you have lost along the way. We hope you will regain your strength in your journey with us. We hope that you will come to enjoy your life, even if your adolescent is making poor decisions. Most of all, our mission is to help whipped parents, so talk shows can find a new topic to focus on and we can all keep our dignity and respect.

— Kimberly Abraham, MSW, CSW

CHAPTER ONE

The Whipped Parent

Welcome to The Whipped Parent Club. There's no fee. As a whipped parent you've already paid plenty of dues — emotional and financial. There are only two qualifications to be a member of this club. First, you must be the parent of a rebellious adolescent. Second, you must be whipped — exhausted, confused and at a loss for what to try next. If you see yourself at all in the opening poem (see p. vi), you're an automatic member of the club.

But wait . . . there's a twist. The Whipped Parent Club is different from any other club. We're unique. That's because we actually want to *lose* our members. When you pick up this book, you see yourself as a whipped parent. As you journey with us through each chapter, we hope you'll no longer identify yourself as "whipped." Sure, you'll probably still have a challenging adolescent. But you'll no longer be disheartened and exhausted. You'll be well on your way to regaining your emotional well-being.

Are You Putting Up with CRAP?

Based on our experience as both parents and therapists, we've developed a unique approach to deal with challenging adolescents. This book is based on that approach. Parents we've worked with have typically had the same thing to say about life with a defiant, angry teen: "This is crap." And they couldn't be more correct. These adolescents are **C**hildren **R**ebelling **A**gainst **P**arenting (**CRAP**), so the technique we've developed to deal with this type of child is similarly called the **C**oncrete **R**ational **A**pproach to **P**arenting (**CRAP**).

This parenting approach is different from any other because it focuses on the overwhelmed and frustrated parent who is trying to raise a defiant, combative and maybe even violent adolescent to maturity. It's for the *whipped* parent who is often judged unfairly. It's for you, the frazzled parent, who has tried it all and still has a child who doesn't seem to care about you, your rules or your expectations — let alone those of society. It's for parents who put up with *crap* every day.

Throughout this book, we'll use examples of adolescents and parents with whom we've worked. Although names and identifying information have been changed to protect client confidentiality, these stories are all based in truth. They will help you realize that you are not alone. Many parents wake up with dread each day because they know their child will surely bring conflict and chaos to their home. The following three stories will begin to show how a caring parent can become a "whipped parent."

The Whippets

Meet the Whippets. They are the parents of twelve-year-old Slug Whippet, who won't get up in the morning and go to school. The Whippets are a middle-class family that can afford to provide a good life for Slug and his nine-year-old half-sister. Slug has his own phone, his own television, and all of the newest video games.

Mrs. Whippet is an extremely anxious and disheartened parent. The principal of the school called her earlier in the year and told her that if Slug continued to miss school, *she* would be prosecuted for educational neglect. As his parent, she can be held responsible for his attendance.

The problem is, she can't get him out of bed.

Every school morning Slug's mother wades through his pile of expensive playthings, dirty clothes, and crusty food dishes to wake Slug up for school. She's tried everything she can think of to fix this "getting up for school" problem. She's taken away possessions and privileges, but he just shrugs and says, "So what?" She's tried begging, threatening and crying. Yet when Slug feels like it, which is often, he refuses to get out of bed. Being a rather large boy of twelve, Slug's size and strength give him the advantage. His mother has offered him just about anything if he would just put in the legally required number of days at school. She's tried appealing to his emotional side. With pain in her voice and tears in her eyes, she has asked him if he loves her. Would he really let his own mother be prosecuted rather than get up and go to school?

Slug does everything he can think of to lead his mother on.

Slug often promises his mother that he will go to school tomorrow; but when it comes time to get up the next morning, he just rolls over. Slug does follow some household rules and goes to bed by 9:30 p.m. (after a lot of complaining). Mrs. Whippet has bought Slug his own alarm clock, and she sets it for him every night. Ten minutes after his alarm is shut off, she comes into his room and wakes him again to remind him that it's time to get up. Slug says he is either too sick, too tired or just can't get up.

Sometimes he doesn't even bother to give a reason.

Fed up, his mother finds herself yelling and threatening. "If it weren't for the fact I could be charged with child abuse, Slug, I'd give you a good attitude adjustment. That's what you really need." When all nonviolent tactics fail — and Mrs. Whippet is past the point of caring whether or not her son calls Protective Services — she pulls his hair, slaps his head, and kicks his foot in frustration. All she gets is a handful of hair and some nasty name-calling from her son.

He remains in bed, and she's totally whipped.

Mr. Whippet married Slug's mother when Slug was two years old.

Whenever Mr. Whippet tries to get involved, Slug threatens to become physical. Slug is quick to remind Mr. Whippet that, even though he adopted him as a toddler and Slug was given his last name, Mr. Whippet is *not* his real father and can't tell him what to do. Because such scenes cause the entire family trauma and only make the already stressful situation worse, Mr. Whippet no longer tries to intervene.

Mrs. Whippet loves her son, but she doesnít understand him.

He keeps his body very clean but lives in a filthy room. He is an intelligent boy, yet his teachers say that he is capable of doing much better, and he is failing most of his classes due to truancy. He is quick-tempered, and his mother is just a little bit afraid of him . . . and his mouth. He uses the worst language she's ever heard, even though she and Mr. Whippet rarely swear. Slug's mother feels hopelessly controlled by her son. She is giving up, becoming depressed, and she doesn't know what she can do about it. Mr. Whippet has even considered leaving the marriage. They are whipped parents.

Mrs. Booker

Meet Thelma Booker, a hardworking single parent. Her daughter, Brandy Booker, is an adolescent who doesn't care what others want her to do. She cares even less about what anyone thinks of her, particularly her mother. Brandy walks down the street in her seductive clothes. Her long dark hair frames a ghostly white face that is set off in black, from heavy eye liner down to her lipstick. You would never guess that she is only thirteen.

Brandy is completely self-centered.

She is snooty, snotty, and usually has poor hygiene. She proudly flaunts nose and tongue rings. Her hobby is to practice black magic. She attends school regularly but doesn't do her homework or care about her grades. Brandy doesn't have any respect for her mother and she refuses to do any chores around the house. Ms. Booker says, "Brandy is a liar, a thief, and she shows the world nothing but hate. Besides that, she smells bad."

Brandy is what Ms. Booker refers to as a "parent abuser. î If her mother tries to control her in any way or gives her *a hard time,* Brandy is likely to hit and push. She throws temper tantrums and uses abusive language. Most of the time Brandy ignores her mother or treats her like she's something stuck on the bottom of her shoe. She comes and goes as she pleases.

She follows the house rules or gives her mother the time of day only when she wants something.

The law says, and Brandy is quick to remind her mother, that Ms. Booker could be prosecuted for child abuse if she uses physical force to control or punish Brandy. Or as Brandy puts it, "If you ever try to lay a fat-ass hand on me." Yet legally, society holds Ms. Booker responsible for Brandy's behavior because she is a minor. Once, when the police brought a sulking Brandy home because she was out past the city curfew, the officer told Ms. Booker she would be fined if Brandy was caught out after curfew again. Short of tying her up (it's a one-story house, and Brandy has a habit of sneaking out her bedroom window), Ms. Booker doesn't see what she can do.

She feels she is in a lose-lose situation ó with no control.

She says she's to the point of hating her daughter. Ms. Booker is a *whipped* parent.

Top Dog Rules

Meet Top Dog's mother. Top Dog is a seventeen-year-old alcoholic and drug addict.

Top Dogís mother says she cries herself to sleep every night.

Her son started using marijuana when he was twelve years old. By the time he was fifteen, he was using alcohol and marijuana almost daily. He's been in many severe, life-threatening fights, often with men several years older than he is. Some he won and bragged about later. Some he lost, coming home beaten and bloody. Recently, Top Dog added cocaine to his drugs of choice. Top Dog always turns angry and violent when drinking alcohol. Now, with the help of cocaine, he can drink even greater amounts of alcohol without passing out.

Top Dog's mother describes the time that she was called by the hospital emergency staff.

They told her Top Dog had been admitted for head trauma and a severely gashed face, which required stitches. They told her he was being taken upstairs for a CAT scan to rule out brain injuries. As Top Dog's mother listened on the other end of the line, things started to go black. She became too hot, and knew she was going to pass out. The vision of him all cut and bloody added to the fears she already had for her son's life. She slid to the floor and lay there on the cold tile, trying to stay conscious so she could listen to the rest of the information.

The nurse told her that Top Dog was intoxicated and had been brought to the emergency room by ambulance. He was being obnoxious, and he wanted to leave the hospital without getting his stitches or the results of the CAT scan. The nurse went on to say that he really needed to stay until they determined how severe his injuries were. He had been in a fight at a party and had received several beer-bottle blows to the head and face. He was at risk of losing an eye.

Top Dog's mom receives many phone calls like this because Top Dog is a fighter.

He often engages in dangerous, life-threatening fights.

A year prior to Top Dog's use of cocaine, his four best friends were killed in a tragic car accident. It was one of the few times he wasn't with them. The driver and all three passengers were highly intoxicated. They were traveling at a speed exceeding one hundred miles an hour when their car became airborne.

Top Dog has been checked into drug rehabilitation programs twice before, but the treatments didn't last. His mother has threatened to make him move out of her home if he doesn't stop using. She begs, pleads, bargains and bribes, trying to make him understand how much he is hurting her and the entire family. Nothing works.

She is guilt-ridden because she can't figure out what to do to help her son stop using drugs. That is the root of her problem. *There isn't anything she can do.* It's up to Top Dog, and he continues to choose to use.

Top Dog's mother knows only too well the fear that parents go through when they're raising this type of adolescent. Her constant worry has caused her hair to start falling out.

She has become physically ill, and she is an emotional wreck.

She lives each day in constant fear of what might happen to her son next. She pictures horror after horror, with all the gory details of blood and guts. She's terrified of how she will live through it if he is ever permanently injured or killed. She always prepares for the worst, and even routinely rehearses his funeral in her mind. Top Dog's mother is terrified and depressed. She is a *whipped* parent.

Are You a Whipped Parent?

Do these families' stories sound at all familiar? If they do, you need to realize that, more than anything you may have said or done, your situation may very well be the simple result of a roll of nature's genetic dice.

You may bring both Jack and Jill into this world, feed them, clothe them, love them and raise them the same, with hopes that they will each reward you with love and kindness in return. From the very first day, you may shower each of them with love, provide for their basic needs, and try to teach them good, solid rules to live by.

Jill may be sugar, spice and everything nice, while Jack is the poster child for defiance. One morning, you may need a bucket of water from the top of the hill behind your house. If you hand the bucket to Jill, you can be sure she will take it from you with a smile, give you a peck on the cheek and return minutes later with a full bucket of water. Not a drop will be spilled along the way. Try the same thing with Jack, and he will tell you to get your own water — he has better things to do. (You wouldn't get far with Slug because he won't get up that early in the morning. Brandy would hit you in the shins with the bucket, and Top Dog would take the bucket from you and trade it in for a pack of cigarettes halfway up the hill.)

You Are a Motivated Reader

You bought this book for a reason: you don't like the way you're feeling. You can probably identify with at least one of these emotions:

- anger
- pain
- disappointment
- embarrassment
- sadness
- stress
- fear
- exhaustion
- guilt

You may even be feeling all of the above *and* overwhelmed. You probably live with an adolescent who is similar to Slug, Brandy or Top Dog. You may feel as though your adolescent controls you, your family and your home. You've been given suggestions on how to *control* your child by teachers, therapists, friends, your parent(s), spouse, lover and the woman in line behind you at the grocery store. Nothing has worked. Now you've picked up this book. Maybe someone suggested that you read it, and your first thought going into it may be, "Yeah, right. This is going to be one *more* thing that won't work."

The techniques in this book may or may not promote change in your adolescent. They will, however, promote changes within *you*. You will come away knowing you have provided every opportunity for your teen to change, if he chooses to do so. These techniques *work* because *you* will regain your emotional strength.

The CRAP Approach Can Help

We work exclusively with parents whose adolescents have severe emotional and behavioral problems. Many of those parents initially come to us feeling helpless and hopeless. However, we've used the CRAP approach both individually and in groups, and parents who have attended groups based on CRAP tell us that it *does* work. They *feel better*. That's what we hope this book does for you — make you feel better.

What Makes the CRAP Technique Different?

CRAP is different than techniques developed by other professionals. Almost all others try to teach parents how to *regain control and authority over an adolescent*. We'll tell you why controlling tactics and unrealistic expectations are the key reasons that parents become angry, frustrated, overwhelmed and exhausted. This is especially true when an adolescent doesn't fit into society's picture of how he should be.

- We'll show you how to *recognize the emotional buttons your teen may use to control you*, including anger, guilt and embarrassment.

- We'll also teach you how to *change your reactions to your childís tactics*, so you can regain control over your own emotions.

CRAP was designed for you, the *whipped* parent. We hope you enjoy your journey with us. We hope you find strength, encouragement and emotional well-being. As a bonus, we'll do our best to help you find those times during which you can actually enjoy raising the type of kid, like Jack, who can whip the best of us.

CHAPTER TWO

Changing Times

The reasons people decide to have children have changed over time. In *the old days*, children were actually needed. They were an important part of a family's financial survival. Children, especially adolescents, helped their parents by working on the family farm. Many worked outside of the home, in mines or in factories. Girls cared for the younger children in a family and did a large part of the housekeeping. A child's role was different than that of today. Back then, he made important contributions to the family.

Over the years, our country changed dramatically. The industrial revolution created more job opportunities for people, with higher wages. The role children played in the family started to change. We no longer needed the contributions from our children for survival. Society and the government put laws in place to protect children from long work hours. Education became a "right," and a child's job was no longer to work but to go to school.

Why We Have Children

Today, children are more often born in response to the emotional needs of a parent: "I (or we) *want* to have a baby." Sure, there are still times when pregnancies occur accidentally — just like in the old days.

But in this *modern time*, people can choose whether to parent that infant or place him for adoption. They can even choose to end the pregnancy. Those who choose to have a baby, and parent him, do so based on some type of emotion.

So even if a pregnancy is not deliberate, the choice to parent a baby is. There is no logical reason to have a child. Think about it. Can you come up with one logical reason to have children? They cost a lot of money, and they're typically messy. They take a toll on our homes and our lives in general. They do bring us happiness, but they also give us grief. Ultimately, a child's role in the family today is to fill the emotional needs of a parent.

The Emotions of New Parents

Emotion is a powerful thing. The phrase "love is blind" didn't come out of nowhere. When you choose to have (or parent) a child, you're often stuck in the *good* emotions. You believe it will be a wonderful experience to have a baby to care for and love. What fun it will be to buy baby clothes and decorate a nursery. How rewarding it will be to watch that child grow into a successful adult. The love and nurturing you give him will come back to you in so many ways.

If the decision were based in logic, people probably wouldn't take on the role of parenting. You never thought to yourself,

> *Boy, a kid can cost a lot of cash. I might have the type of child who wonít listen, wonít do what I tell him and who will fight with other kids. The school could call me every week to chastise me for having a disruptive child in their classroom. He might steal from me, destroy my house and join a gang. And Iíll be held responsible for all of it. My neighbors could end up hating me and gossiping about what a bad parent I am. My family will shame me for not raising my child right. He could swear at me, tell me he hates me and make me feel guilty for not giving him enough. Iíll spend endless nights worrying about what heís doing.*

We go into parenting with hopes and dreams. We have high expectations about what our child will be like and how we will be as parents. Society holds us to those expectations, long after we realize that they were unrealistic. The thing is, a child doesn't come with a remote control. You can't push a button and have him respond to your command. He isn't an object that can be programmed. He's a human being, born with his own mind and personality. When you decide to have a child, it's a *crap-shoot*. Conception is a roll of the genetic dice, and what comes about is chance.

The Modern Teen

Children today grow up with a higher need for instant gratification than any previous generation. They've come to expect it; even demand it. Computers, televisions, cars. Things that once were worked toward as a goal for the entire family are now usually provided for children by financially capable parents. This has snowballed with the "normal" self-centeredness that is part of adolescence. We've created a "me first" generation.

Some teenagers believe parents should provide for them all that their little hearts desire. Especially material things. Since we have children out of our own emotional needs, it's no wonder we're disheartened when they don't treat us in the way we expected. They value the opinions of their peers and the media more than what we have to say. They seem to spend the entire day doing the exact opposite of what we want them to do. Our emotional needs aren't always fulfilled.

The Emotions of a Whipped Parent

As human beings, we are constantly experiencing emotions: happiness, excitement, sadness, fear, anger, shame, guilt and disappointment. People have a range of emotions every day, often more than one at a time. When you're the parent of a challenging adolescent, it can seem like the emotions you feel the most are those that are uncomfortable, unpleasant or terrifying. And that's probably true. Parents become *whipped* when they are constantly bombarded by negative feelings that leave them disheartened, and sometimes feeling hopeless.

Whoís to Blame
When Kids Go Bad?

During the past decade, there has been an increasing focus on violence among youth. Recently, the severity of school violence has led to an intense, nationwide scrutiny of the crimes committed by children. When an adult commits a crime, he or she is typically held responsible for the action by society and its laws. But when a child or adolescent engages in the same behavior, the tendency is to look for an adult who is at fault for the crime, especially if violence is involved.

As a society, we have a hard time accepting that children and adolescents may be violent. We want to view childhood as a time of innocence, and violence doesn't fit with that picture. If a twelve year old physically assaults a classmate, who is accountable for that act? If a thirteen year old chooses to sell drugs, who is ultimately responsible for that decision? If a fourteen year old refuses to attend school, who should be prosecuted?

The focus often comes to rest on a child's parents, and people point to the type of upbringing that was present. Do the parents take the child to church, help him with his homework, set rules and enforce them? Do the parents monitor his television shows, listen to him and spend time with him? Do they do all the things that *good* parents are supposed to do? *Surprise.* The answer to these questions is often *yes.* Many children and adolescents who come from what appears to be "good homes" still make bad choices, push against everyone and everything, and even commit crimes.

Society has sent the message, loud and clear, that parents are responsible for their child's behavior. The definition of a *responsible parent* has changed over the years. Responsibility to feed, clothe, shelter and love your child was the old days. Today, you're held responsible for how your child behaves, what he says, what he looks like and how he *turns out*. If your adolescent breaks the law, you'd better hire a good lawyer. Not for him — for you. You're the one society will want to prosecute. Just read the latest poll from any newspaper or talk show. If a kid is violent or commits a crime, the first and loudest question asked is "Where were the parents?" If you have an answer, you may as well save your breath. It won't be good enough.

Society

These new expectations placed on parents today are completely unrealistic. They're at the core of what is leaving so many parents emotionally sick. As a bonus, society's expectations only contribute to this generation's struggles. Normal adolescence is a time to break free from parents and become independent. You did it. I did it. Our parents did it and so did theirs. Parents today are fearful of loosening their grip because society says "hang on tight." Teens today end up fighting harder, and often more recklessly, to break free.

Even more damaging is the reality that these adolescents probably won't be held responsible for their own negative or illegal behavior. Why should an adolescent change his behavior when his parents are the ones who experience the consequences? It's a lot easier to act up or commit crimes if you figure someone else will pay the price.

Those who are quick to blame the parents for a child's actions fail to take into account that every child is born with a personality. Some humans are born with tendencies to be compliant and sensitive, and they accept the opinions and limits of society. Others may be naturally inclined toward noncompliance, self-interest and aggression, and they have little or no regard for society's expectations. You, as a parent, are subject to the whims of nature. You may be fortunate enough to have the first type of child. You're in for a lot of personal growth if you have the second kind.

Thereís Hope

This book can help you find your emotional well-being, without relying on your adolescent to help you get there. We know you are under tremendous pressure from society. School officials, neighbors, police, family and therapists all have opinions. Some are quick to point the finger of blame . . . usually at you. It can become mind-boggling. We'll help you look at parenting in a concrete, rational way. We'll give you tools you can use to protect yourself when your child fails to fall in line with society's expectations, rules and laws. We'll help you feel better.

CHAPTER THREE

HELP!
My Kid's Out of Control

Many Americans seem to believe that parents can actually control their children, at least until they become adults. Because of this belief, society and its laws hold parents responsible for their child's actions until their child has reached the age of eighteen. But those of us who have the type of child who rebels against being controlled recognize that this is an impossible and unfair expectation. Impossible, because you simply can't control another person who refuses to be controlled. It doesn't matter if he's eight, eighteen or eighty. Unfair, because the only way someone can *try* to control another person who is adamantly fighting against being controlled is to physically force them into it. As you can probably guess, if a parent uses physical force against a child, society will label it abuse.

The Control Myth

Control plays a big part in the lives of many parents. Whipped parents have been told over and over again that they need to control their child's behavior. Even the definition of control found in The *New Britannica-Webster Dictionary & Reference Guide* (1988) supports the idea that parents can control a child:

. . . to exercise restraining or directing influence over; REGULATE (*control* one's temper) . . . to have power over; RULE (*control* a territory) . . . the power or authority to *control* or command (**children under their parentís** *control)* . . . ability to control (lose *control* of a car) . . .

Notice the examples that were used in that definition to show what it means to have control: temper, territory, a car and *children.* Children are the only human beings mentioned in reference to being controlled. Not neighbors, friends, employees, husbands, wives or other relatives. Why are children considered to be different? Because they aren't adults?

Have you ever seen someone in the grocery store try to control their two-year-old child who doesn't want to be controlled? You know, the one who's laying on the floor screaming and kicking his feet. Mom's yelling, "Stand up right now!" Does he ever really stand on his feet? No! Mom picks him up, and carries him out of the store, still kicking and screaming. He had the ultimate control over not standing up. The only control she had was taking him out of the store, since he was still small enough for her to pick up. Who do you think controlled the situation? Mom had to leave — without the groceries.

Your adolescent is not a car, or a territory, or anything else that you have "control" over. He's a person, just like you, your neighbor, and the frustrating co-worker who gets on your nerves. It doesn't matter that he's under eighteen years old. It doesn't matter that you are his parent and helped give him life (or chose to adopt him). Plus, he's too big for you to carry, kicking and screaming, out of a store.

The dictionary is correct to use inhuman objects and concepts, like a car, to illustrate control, but wrong to imply that another human being can be controlled. If we're sitting in a room, and I want you to get up, drive to the store and buy me a Coca-Cola, I can't *make* you do it. I can control my own behavior and hope it influences you. I may offer you money or your own soda, ask nicely and offer to return the favor sometime, look sad and beg because I'm so thirsty, or even nastily threaten you if you refuse. But no matter how I choose to behave, the ultimate control over whether or not you drive to the store and get me a Coke is in *your* hands — not mine.

Your adolescent will make his choices no matter what you say or do. He may choose to listen to your suggestions, but ultimately the decisions he makes are under his control.

Nothing you can do will change that. You can tell your child, "You need to go to school to get an education and be successful in this world. If you don't go to school, you'll be truant and may end up in trouble with the court." Some kids may hear you, and decide, "Yeah, okay, I hate school, but I gotta go." Others may hear you and decide, "Yeah? So what? I hate school, and I'm still not going!" In the end, the decision each makes is under his control, and the consequences need to be his problem. The only thing you can control is the way you choose to respond to your child's behavior.

Give It Up

The foundation of CRAP is the ability to think in a **C**oncrete, **R**ational manner.

ACCEPTING THE FACT THAT THE ONLY PERSON YOU CAN TRULY CONTROL IS YOURSELF, AND THAT YOU CANNOT CONTROL A CHILD WHO REFUSES TO BE CONTROLLED, IS PART OF CONCRETE, RATIONAL THINKING.

There, we've said it. It's in print. In capital letters. What's your reaction? We know that, in asking you to accept this, we're asking you to take a leap of faith. The idea that you can't control your child is a frightening idea to most people. Why? Because loss of control is a scary thing. When it's in relation to your child, whom you love and have been told for years that you should control, it's terrifying.

Raising a child can be like riding in a car that your child controls because *he is the driver.* You are a passenger and probably a backseat driver. You can tell your child: "You're almost out of gas!" "Watch out for that pothole!" "There's a detour in the road up there!" "You need to take the next exit!" "You're speeding — slow down!"

However, your child has the ultimate control over the accelerator, steering wheel, gear shift and brakes. You can't *make* him take your suggestions. He may choose not to get off at the next exit and get fuel. As a result, he may or may not run out of gas. He may choose not to avoid the pothole. As a result he may get a flat tire. He can speed, and he may get a ticket. Because he has the control, it's his choice. He probably already knows which choice *you'd* like him to make. That doesn't mean he will make the choice *you want.* Some people, especially adolescents, like to push things to the limit to learn for themselves just how far they can go before they actually run out of gas.

If you always point out, "Your gas gauge is on low fuel — you'd better stop," your adolescent will not learn to keep an eye on the gas gauge himself. He'll know that you will tell him, probably several times. If you continually tell your child what choices to make, he will have trouble practicing how to make decisions for himself. He may make mistakes with his own choices, but that's how he'll learn. He may have to run out of gas a few times before he starts reading the fuel gauge.

You can alert your child to the possible consequences of the choices he or she is making:

- "Smoking is dangerous to your health."
- "If you don't get a diploma, it may be hard to get a job."
- "If you have unprotected sex, you could end up with a baby or a disease."

However, the choice is ultimately up to your child. You cannot *make* him behave in the way you or society feel he should. Wanting your child to go to college or even finish high school are good examples of *exit*s you'd like your child to take on the highway of life. He may or may not choose to do so, and he controls the steering wheel. The thing to remember is, expressways go both ways, and an exit missed may be returned to at a later time in life. However, that will be up to your child and will happen only if that is a goal of *his ó* not yours.

Along for the Ride

When society holds a parent responsible for an adolescent's behavior, it's based on the premise that a parent can control the child. This is similar to giving the parent a ticket if their adolescent is speeding. Remember, you are only a passenger. No matter how much you instruct, beg, plead or nag, your child has ultimate control over where that car goes. This book will help you learn how to work with community agencies, including the school, police and court, to ensure that you're not the one who pays the ticket.

Your child's driving skills may not be great, but he's the one who must practice strengthening them. *He is the one who must decide if his actions are worth the price he may have to pay.* You can improve only your own responses to his choices. If your child continues to ignore your suggestions on how to strengthen his skills, you may choose not to go along for the ride. You might say, "You know what? You keep choosing to shoplift, against my suggestions, and that's illegal behavior. I'm not going to be a part of that. I think I'll let you take this particular ride alone."

As you ride with your child through adolescence, there will be people in cars in the lane next to you who may look at you critically:

- "God, your kid's an awful driver!"
- "Can't you make him slow down?"
- "Your kid needs to wash his car!"
- "Why did your kid drive over that huge pothole?"
- "Can't you control his driving?"

Remember, you can only control yourself, not your child's choices, and other drivers often look in the lane next to them when they should be keeping their eyes on the road in front of them.

CRAP was designed to help you learn how to change your own behavior and reactions, in the hope that you can develop peace of mind for yourself. Hopefully, such changes will also have a positive impact on your adolescent. At the very least, if your child continues to make choices that appear destructive, you will learn how to take care of yourself. You'll no longer feel that your adolescent controls you, your family and your home. Our techniques will help you change from being a whipped parent to one who is secure in the knowledge that you are doing all that you can do.

The Whipped Parentís Serenity Prayer
by Marney Studaker-Cordner

God, grant me the serenity to accept the things I cannot change,
The courage to change the things I can,
And the strength not to kill my kid!

CHAPTER FOUR

I Never Expected This

Jack and Jill, oh what a thrill, the day that each was born.
Jack fell short of his parents hopes
While Jill fulfilled their dreams.

*A*n *expectation* is something you *assume* will happen. Everyone has expectations for the other people in their lives, and it's often taken for granted that an expectation will be met. You may expect that your spouse or lover will be faithful, that your neighbor will respect your property, and that your friend won't criticize you to others. Every day you're placed in a situation where you or someone else is confronted with an expectation.

Expectations are a very big part of the relationship between a parent and child. Whether you are pleased or disappointed in your child's behavior is tied to how well that child is living up to your expectations. Have you ever caught yourself thinking or even saying to your child, "I'm so disappointed in you"? That disappointment comes from him falling short of one of your expectations. In the back of your mind, the thought may be, *What kind of parent will people think I am?* That's because parents typically believe their child's behavior is a reflection of themselves.

Believe it or not, your child is *not* a reflection of you. To think so is self-centered. Your adolescent's life is about *him* — not you. His mistakes and successes are his own, just as yours belong to you.

What Do You Expect?

How do you know when you have an expectation? A good clue is if you find yourself saying or thinking something close to, "Julie will always . . . Jason needs to . . . if Jill would just . . . my son will . . . my daughter will not . . . " If you feel angry, frustrated or disappointed because your teenager won't do what you believe he should do, it's a safe bet you've got an expectation that's not being met.

The aggravating part about having an expectation for someone else is that you have such limited control over whether or not the expectation gets met.

Brandy Booker's mom once said: "I give Brandy respect, and I *expect* she'll respect me."

(Uh-huh, so does she?)

"NO. She constantly swears in front of me, which is totally disrespectful and unacceptable. *She needs to stop.*"

(Uh-huh, and how can you control what she says?)

"Well, I could . . . I could . . . I guess I really can't."

(Right.)

That's because Brandy is the only one who has control over Brandy's mouth. Even if you got the masking tape out and taped her mouth shut, she'd just pull it off. Then she'd probably head to the phone and hit the speed-dial to Protective Services for child abuse.

Expectations Set You Up for Disappointment

If Ms. Booker continues to *expect* that Brandy will respect her and stop swearing, she will continue to set herself up to be disappointed. Expectations set you up for disappointment. That's because Mrs. Booker's expectation is ultimately under Brandy's control.

If you get married and figure you'll never get divorced, there are two parts to that expectation: 1) you will not file for divorce, and 2) your spouse will not file for divorce. You can control the first part, but your spouse controls the second half of that expectation. Ultimately, he or she controls their own behavior and whether or not to file for divorce. Have you ever heard someone (maybe yourself) say, "I never expected I'd be this age and divorced (or single, widowed or unemployed)"? Expectations aren't always met in life.

The Evolution of Expectations

Our children are the ones for whom we tend to have the most expectations. There's a picture somewhere in your mind of how you'd like your child to "turn out." Your expectations are formed around that picture. You aren't usually aware of all the expectations you have until you stop and consciously think about them. That's what we're going to do now.

First, please understand that expectations are different from hopes. An expectation is something you think of as a *necessary* prospect for the future. It's something you believe *has* to happen. You're counting on it. A hope is something you *want* or *wish* for. You can hope that your child is happy, healthy and lives to a ripe old age. Hopes are okay. Expectations are dangerous.

Just how do you end up with an expectation? Here are a few ways:

- Those hopes and dreams you had for your child turned into expectations.

- You expect your child to do something you wish you had done yourself.

- You acted or felt a certain way and now expect your child to act or feel the same.

- Society's expectations became yours.

- Expectations handed down through generations of your family became yours.

When You Wish Upon a Star . . .

Some expectations begin as hopes or dreams. When you first hold your tiny new baby, you start having hopes and dreams for that child. You dream about the kind of person he'll be, what his life will be like, and how proud you'll feel as a parent. Hopes and dreams may form before a baby is born or even conceived. If your baby was planned, you probably spent some time thinking about why you wanted a child. You had some hopes. Children are often brought into this world today because of a parent's emotional needs. Brandy's mom once said, "I always wanted a daughter. I thought we'd go shopping, and spend time together. I thought we'd be close. It ended up we can't even be in the same room for more than a few minutes without arguing. I never thought it would be this way."

It's hard to hold that little human being and not dream about what he'll do in his life. There are so many possibilities. The problem comes when what started out as a hope or dream turns into an expectation. Remember Slug? Before he turned five, Slug's mother dreamed about him going to college. This dream gradually turned into an expectation, something Mrs. Whippet counted on. She wasn't prepared that Slug would hate his teachers and simply not care about his education. Remember how she felt when Slug refused to get up in the morning and she was threatened with educational neglect? To say she was disappointed is putting it mildly. The expectation that her son would go to school wasn't just because of the legal issue. It was also born from a hope created in her own heart and mind. It didn't have any connection to *the reality of who Slug is.*

You may *hope* your child will be healthy. That hope may become an *expectation* that your child won't do anything harmful to his body, like smoking or doing drugs. You may *hope* that your child loves you. That may become an *expectation* that your child will be thoughtful and considerate of your feelings. In either case, you may be disappointed.

Take a minute and think back to those first hopes and dreams you had for your child. Have any of them turned into expectations?

Do as I Say, Not as I Did

Some expectations are the hopes and dreams that parents had for themselves. You may want your child to do the things you always wished you had done. These may be expectations you had for *yourself* that went unmet. Slug's mother had planned to go to college. Instead, she got pregnant, had to drop out and go to night school, just to finish high school. Her dream for Slug to go to college is exactly that: *her* dream.

Wanting a "better life" for your child than you feel you had yourself is a very common hope. You will know that hope has turned into an expectation if you find yourself saying something like, "I never got to go to college. I worked in the shop all my life. All these years I've worked overtime so my son won't have to work a blue-collar job. I can send him to college, and he'll have a better life than I did."

Your *hope* may become the *expectation* that your adolescent will learn from your mistakes. You expect he'll take you up on the opportunities you make available to him. Fourteen-year-old Target's father pointed his finger at him in a therapy session and said, "I was an alcoholic for ten years, and you will *not* go through the same thing." Target was already drinking regularly. He kept doing so, despite his father's expectation that he would quit. Target's dad became angry, disappointed and frustrated. His expectation that his son's life would be different from his own wasn't being met, and he had no control over that.

Think about what you were like as a teenager. Did you get into trouble? Many parents who have kids like Jack were pretty rowdy themselves, back in *their* day. It's natural to hope your child will make different choices in *his* day. You can't count on it, though. Jack has to learn the same way you did: by making his own choices.

Today society reacts much more strongly to the same adolescent behaviors that were considered typical just a generation ago. Mrs. Whippet remembers getting pulled over by the police several times as a teenager. On one occasion, she and three friends were out "cruising." They had a twelve-pack of Busch beer on the floor of the front seat. The driver had just taken a drag off the joint Mrs. Whippet had rolled. There was marijuana on the dashboard. They were going ten miles over the speed limit, down a back road. You name it, they reeked of it. The cop that pulled them over had them pour out the beer, then he followed them home to make sure they got there in one piece. He didn't say a thing to their parents. Today Mrs. Whippet would be in a detention cell next to Top Dog. People would be saying, "Where were her parents?" Yet Mrs. Whippet has always *expected* her son Slug to "stay out of trouble."

Take a minute to think about the expectations you have for your adolescent. Are some of them ones you wish you'd met yourself? Your teenager may not have the same dreams or expectations for himself, and that's okay. This is *his day* to decide what he expects of himself and to follow his own hopes and dreams.

I Did It, and So Should You

Expectations may be born out of your own life experiences. You followed your parents' rules and never thought of sneaking out of the house. You never swore in front of your parents. You never broke the law by shoplifting. You may have smoked marijuana, but you never did any "harder" drugs. You got a job when you were seventeen. Without even realizing it, you may *expect* your adolescent to follow in your footsteps. But your shoes may not fit him.

Sometimes parents even expect their adolescent's personality to be like their own. Thirteen-year-old Spice never cared how her behavior affected other people. She stole her mom's keys and took her new car for a joy ride. She missed a curve and ended up in the ditch. Her mom couldn't understand why Spice showed no remorse for her behavior, saying, "When I was growing up, all my mom had to do was tell me she was disappointed in me, and I was in tears. But Spice doesn't care if I'm disappointed in her or if she makes me sad or mad as hell.

My son is just like me. If I just frown at him, he stops what he's doing because he wants to make me happy. I just don't understand Spice. She's not *turning out* the way I thought she would."

Spice's mom has to accept the fact that her daughter's personality is different from her own. By expecting Spice to have the same feelings and behaviors as she and her son do, Spice's mom is setting herself up for continual disappointment.

Think about the life experiences you've had. Have you turned any of those choices or personal traits into expectations for your adolescent? He may march to the beat of his own drum. In fact, he may not even be in the same band as you.

What Will Other People Think?

Society's expectations sometimes become yours. There are all sorts of expectations in our society. Society makes it clear what those expectations are, and most of them are called laws. People generally expect that others will obey laws. Some adolescents break the law by running away from home, being physically assaultive, refusing to go to school, using or dealing drugs, breaking city curfew or stealing. Such adolescents are failing to live up to societal expectations.

When Jack breaks the law, the message he sends to society is, "I don't care what anyone thinks I should do. I'm going to do things my way anyway." Most adolescents are very aware of what society's expectations are — some just don't care. Others care but want to take the risk and hope they can get away with it. Society sets up consequences for breaking the law, such as juvenile detention, probation, residential or foster care placement. The thought of these consequences may leave Jill feeling uncomfortable or scared enough to live up to society's expectations. Jack, however, may push against those expectations by continuing to break the law.

Other societal expectations aren't put into laws. Society expects most people will work or do something in life considered "productive." Top Dog may choose to work only enough to get money for alcohol and drugs. Adolescents often push against society's expectation that people will be polite and tactful. They *tell it like it is*. Have you ever been mortified when your teenager looks at someone, usually another adult like a teacher or family friend, and says something like, "Mind your own business" or "Shut up"? Jill may be very concerned about what other people think, both of her and of you. Jack couldn't care less.

Parents typically have the same expectations for their children that society does, laws or not. It may never have occurred to them that their teenager wouldn't meet those expectations.

Remember, your child is not a reflection of you.

If you continue to believe that he is, you're more likely to want him to change to meet your expectations. You'll want to be "proud" of him, instead of "disappointed."

When you look in the mirror, there's only one reflection you should see: yours.

Thatís the Way Itís Always Been in Our Family

Expectations handed down through generations of your family became yours. It's probably been a generational expectation in your family that kids won't swear at their parents. So when Jack tells you you're "full of shit," you may be shocked, furious and disappointed. Your expectation wasn't met. Ms. Booker says, "My parents are shocked at the way Brandy talks to me." Top Dog's mom says, "In my family, doing drugs is totally unacceptable."

If your family gets together on Christmas Day every year, and it's been that way as long as you can remember, you may expect your children will be there. Jill will probably get up early to help with the meal. Jack will grab a cookie on his way out the door to his girlfriend's house. If you're lucky, he'll say, "See 'ya." You can *hope* he will stick around, but if you *expect* it, you may be disappointed.

When your teenager doesn't live up to generational expectations, it can be especially tough on you, the parent. You may feel the need to explain Jack's behavior to family members, like grandparents, aunts or uncles. You don't have to explain your teen's behavior. That's his job, and he probably wouldn't be bothered to do so.

Generational expectations change because someone in the family was the first to push against them. There was a time when most families had the generational expectation that divorce wasn't acceptable and wouldn't happen. Expectations are *not* always met. People do get divorced. Jill will follow your family's values. Jack will do what he wants. He doesn't care what you or your family think or expect.

Unmet Expectations

Now you've consciously recognized how your expectations came to be. At this point, you may be saying to yourself (and to us), "Wait a minute. This is *my* kid and *my* house. Don't I have the right to expect certain things?"

Yes, Jack is *your* child. You helped give him life (or chose to adopt him). But he's also a human being. He has his own mind, will and personality. Yes, it's *your* house. You absolutely have the right to set limits on how your property will be used and treated. But remember, you can't control Jack.

*You can control only yourself
and your response to Jackís behavior.*

You can set reasonable, realistic expectations for your property and the physical safety of your family. It's up to Jack how he responds to those limits. In Chapter Eleven, you'll learn how to come up with consequences for when Jack doesn't meet those expectations — consequences based on things you *can* control.

Letting Go of Expectations

Keep in mind that you bought this book for a reason. You don't like the way you're feeling. Disappointment and anger related to unmet expectations are a *big* part of that. You can choose to hang onto any or all of your expectations for your child. You may continue to expect and continue to be disappointed when those expectations aren't met. Think about a recent time when you were disappointed or resentful. Did you have an expectation someone didn't meet?

Giving up an expectation does *not* mean you give up your opinion or your personal rights. If you've expected that Jack will not be sexually active, and he keeps having sex, you may choose to give up that expectation. In doing so, you'll stop being constantly disappointed by his choice. It *doesnít* mean you agree with Jack's decision. It *does* mean you recognize that he ultimately has control over that choice. You are changing an expectation back into a hope. This will help you let go of some of the unpleasant feelings you're having.

The idea of letting go of expectations is probably very scary. It can leave you feeling powerless, but only at first. In the long run, you'll feel more confident and in control of *your* life. Your back will stop killing you from lugging around the heavy load of expectations that your kid either can't or won't meet.

Your automatic reaction may be, "If I don't have high expectations for my child, he'll be downright immoral. He'll do anything he wants." Your expectations may influence Jill's choices. Jack *already* does anything he wants, despite your expectation. There's a difference between letting go of unrealistic expectations that your adolescent has failed to meet up to this point and hanging onto realistic expectations related to legal and safety issues. The next chapters will show you how to find that "middle ground" and use the power you *do* have regarding expectations. Believe it or not, you do still have some power.

CHAPTER FIVE

Finding Middle Ground

*L*iving with an out-of-control adolescent can feel like riding in the back seat of a car with a reckless driver in control. Not only is the driver inexperienced, he is a maniac in your eyes. You fear for his life. You fear for your life. Your ride is full of highs and lows. There's anticipation and dread as you speed to the top of a hill. On the way down, you want to vomit, and you pray that you make it to the end of the ride. Middle ground is the part when you actually get to take a look around and see what's happening. The ground is level. There's a sense of relief and even relaxation. "Oh *#@%, that was scary. The ride's almost over, though." Middle ground is where you're actually able to think. You may even enjoy some of the scenery.

The Expectations Road Race

Expectations are a lot like that car ride. Careening ahead at full speed are those expectations your child just can't or won't meet. You know the ones. Those nagging unmet hopes and expectations that leave you feeling disappointed, angry, resentful and full of worry. You've read the first chapters of this book and may have decided, "Boy, they're right. I can't expect anything from my child. As a matter of fact, I should just give up all my hopes for him. He'll never meet them anyway." The highest unmet expectations can be followed by extreme lows. "I used to want my child to go to college and be an engineer. I thought he'd have a nice house and family. But he just refused to go to school. Now I figure he'll probably live in a house that's almost condemned. Even that's a high expectation, because he'll probably be homeless."

Sometimes the higher your expectations are,
the harder you hit coming down from them.

A speeding car ride may be exciting the first time you take one. If the ride never stops, however, you end up being fearful, exhausted, overwhelmed and sick. You can probably picture your kid, sitting in the driver's seat, scaring the daylights out of you and refusing to slow down no matter how hysterical you get. When you're traveling at full speed ahead, the times of high expectations, you're feeling anxious, powerless and fearful. "I want so much for my child. I'm afraid of how his life will turn out — *if* he lives to see his future. I need to keep him from ruining his life." When the car slows down, and your expectations are lowered, you may have given up all hopes and expectations. You feel helpless, depressed and totally whipped. "He'll end up dead or in jail. I'm not even going to open myself up to him emotionally, because he'll only hurt me again with his behavior."

Another type of extreme low is when anger and resentment lead you to sabotage your adolescent. "I hope he does end up in jail for drinking and driving. As a matter of fact, next time he goes out with his buddies, I think I'll tip the cops off about what road he usually takes." Without realizing it, you may even set him up to fail. Your *whipped* emotions are what take you from one extreme to the other.

Extremes

As a whipped parent, finding middle ground is the key to feeling better. Mrs. Whippet went from trying to control Slug to deciding she needed to just give up. The hurt and disappointment she'd felt for years had left her exhausted. "All my fighting and begging never did any good.

If they prosecute me for educational neglect, so what? I can't do anything about it anyway, and Slug sure doesn't care. Why should I care? Jail would be a nice vacation away from my son." *Mrs. Whippet got out of the car and just didnít care anymore. She didnít even wave goodbye to Slug as he sped off.*

Ms. Booker experienced so many negative feelings about Brandy's behavior, she actually started to hate her daughter. She went from one extreme to the other. Instead of doing all she could to keep Brandy from getting into trouble with the police, she started trying to "help" her daughter "finally learn a lesson." She went as far as thinking of ways to set Brandy up so she'd end up on probation. "Sometimes I'll lock the door a little before midnight, hoping she'll be late so I can call the cops. After all she's put me through, she deserves something back. She's not going to change anyway, so she might as well find out now what jail's like." *Ms. Booker got out of the car, flattened one of Brandyís tires on the way by, and headed straight to the nearest pay phone. She alerted the police of Brandyís route and asked them to follow Brandy until she messed up. Then she finished by asking them to severely punish her daughter for her recklessness.*

Top Dog's mother never got to the other extreme. She held onto her belief that there was some way she could stop her son from using drugs and alcohol. Holding firm to her expectations for Top Dog set her up for continual disappointment and great suffering, especially when everything she tried had failed. She was so guilt-ridden and terrified that she became physically ill . . . and Top Dog just kept right-on using. *Top Dogís mother refused to get out of the car no matter how bad the ride got. She continued begging, pleading, bribing and threatening the whole way. She became car sick and feared for her life, but she hung right on, sure that she could do something to get Top Dog to slow down. And if not, she was willing to crash with him. He was her son, after all.*

These parents went from having many unrealistic expectations that they couldn't control to expecting the worst from their children. Mrs. Whippet, who once pictured her son successful and in college, started seeing him as a "loser," probably in jail or living on the street. Ms. Booker resigned herself to the idea that Brandy would be pregnant by the time she was fourteen years old. Top Dog's mom continued to rehearse his funeral.

How to Find Middle Ground

All of these parents were able to identify how their lows were usually followed again by periods of high expectations, much like a rollercoaster ride. Emotions and expectations go up, typically come crashing down, then bounce back up again. Whipped parents just want the ride to stop, but there's no real way to do that with a child. As Ms. Booker once said, "I'd love to tell Brandy she can't live here anymore. But you can't divorce your kid." So if you can't get off the ride, what can you do? Find middle ground. Here's how these folks did it:

Step One

Stop Predicting your childís future. There's no way to predict what his life will be like in his twenties, thirties or beyond. Absolutely none. So stop trying. Picturing his future, especially if you're at one of those highs or lows, will only cause *you* to panic. "Oh my God. He just doesn't care about anything or anyone. He's violent toward his sister. He'll probably end up killing someone someday." Slow down. That's a tremendous leap. *Thereís no way to predict the future.* Whatever you're predicting, good or bad, you're probably wrong.

Step Two

Review. What have you tried with your child so far? Has anything worked? Mrs. Whippet figured out that when she focuses more on her own life, instead of Slug's choice not to go to school, she feels better. Slug is also in a better mood. Ms. Booker realized that, when she doesn't get into verbal conflict with Brandy, after a few minutes her daughter gives up and is able to walk away. She slams the door when she leaves the room, but at least she doesn't get violent. Top Dog's mom couldn't identify anything she's tried with her son that's worked. If you're a parent who has been able to come up with things that work, hang onto those things — even if small — and keep using them.

Step Three

Let go. Once you've identified what has worked with your child in the past, let go of all the things that haven't. If it hasn't worked by now, it's not going to. Why keep traveling down the same old bumpy road?

Step Four

Write down the expectations you can't let go. Decide where each expectation comes from. Is it societal, generational, or maybe one of the other areas we talked about in the last chapter? Keep in mind that letting go of as many expectations as possible will lighten your own load. You will probably want to hang onto more realistic expectations related to legal issues, such as your property, home and the safety of yourself and family members.

Mrs. Whippet decided her expectation that Slug would graduate from high school and then go to college was born mostly out of unfulfilled hopes for herself. However, because he was only thirteen years old, it was also a legal issue for her. She decided to stop expecting him to get up for school, but protected herself from educational neglect (see Chapter Seventeen, "I Left My Sense of Humor on the Courthouse Steps," on schools and how to avoid prosecution). Mrs. Whippet decided she would hang onto her belief that Slug is a smart young man. She will expect that he has the intelligence to use this gift whenever he chooses. In reviewing her expectations, Mrs. Whippet found Slug was already meeting many of them. He wasn't physically violent with peers or his sister. He never stole or destroyed things in her home. She decided to hang onto the expectations she'd taken for granted, ones that Slug was already meeting. *Finding middle ground helped her feel good about herself and her son.*

Ms. Booker decided that her expectation of Brandy to "respect" her came from her first hopes and dreams for Brandy. Society and generational expectations reinforced that Brandy should be respectful. Besides, Ms. Booker had "respected" her own parents, and she expected Brandy to "do as I did." She decided to let go of that expectation. On the other hand, Ms. Booker decided to hang onto her expectation that physical violence would not be tolerated in her home. She realized that, when Brandy hit or shoved her, it became a legal issue that involved the safety of herself and her home. She decided she would phone the police whenever Brandy became assaultive. She let her daughter know she would consistently follow through with that response. *She started to feel relief as she found her middle ground.*

Top Dog's mom wrote down her expectations and found that most of them were for herself. The only expectation she had for her son was that he would stop using drugs and alcohol. She decided to accept the fact that she has no control over Top Dog's choice to use, and that the expectation she had for herself to "make him stop" was unrealistic. Her middle ground was to let him know that she hoped he would make good choices for himself, but to recognize that he had ultimate control over those choices. In regard to expectations for herself, she decided that the only realistic one she would hang on to was that she would attend Al-Anon, a support group for people who have an alcoholic or drug-addicted loved one. *Finding middle ground by taking care of herself helped Top Dog's mom feel healthier.*

Step Five

Provide opportunities. Are you doing everything that you can do to provide opportunities for your adolescent to meet your expectations? When you review what you've already tried with your child, you may realize there are some areas where you can actually do more. Do you respect your adolescent and listen to him without interrupting or automatically arguing? Do you offer to spend time with him, doing something *he* enjoys? Do you find something nice to say to him, at least once a day, despite your anger? Have you continued to let your child know you love him?

Mrs. Whippet got out of the car, feeling confident that Slug was an intelligent boy. She smiled, waved goodbye, and called a friend to pick her up. She let Slug take this particular ride alone. Ms. Booker asked Brandy nicely to stop and let her out of the car. She smiled and wished her daughter a safe ride. Top Dog's mother realized that her life was very important to her. She got out of the car and headed straight for an Al-Anon meeting.

Finding middle ground means finding balance between trying to control things over which you have no control, and going to the other extreme by giving up on or trying to sabotage your adolescent. Expecting your child to fail is as dangerous as having expectations that are too high or unrealistic. You need to continue providing opportunities for him to meet realistic expectations. Even if he doesn't choose to take advantage of the opportunity, you will know you've done all you can do as a parent. The next chapter will show you how to recognize what you can control.

Remember, a race car driver thrives on speed. He loves to push the limits. How well do you think Mario Andretti could drive if his parent were sitting in the back seat of the race car telling him what to do? ¡Mario. Slow down. Watch out, for Godís sake. Oh my God, Mario, youíre crazy.î If you want your adolescent to drive as well as he can, it helps if he doesnít have the distraction of his mother or father constantly back seat driving.

CHAPTER SIX

REALISTIC
Hopes & Expectations

When you live with an out-of-control teen, day after day, it can feel like you have no power or control. The good news is, you do. Just not the way you may have thought. You *can* have realistic hopes and expectations for your adolescent. You *canít* control whether or not he chooses to meet them, but you can provide opportunities for him to do so.

What You *Can* Do

We've already described what you *canít* control. Here's what you *can* do: You can stay on your TOES —

Tell your adolescent what your hope or expectation is.

Opportunity — provide opportunities for him to meet that hope or expectation.

Educate him with knowledge that may help him better decide whether or not to make an effort to meet that expectation.

Show him how to meet that expectation — model it for him.

That's it. Those are the four things you *can* control in relation to the hopes and expectations you have for your adolescent. The common thread in these four steps is that they're based on your own behavior, which you control. The following two pages provide examples of how to use the TOES model with hopes and expectations. You can also use the TOES model to recognize where your power lies, and what you can do in relation to realistic expectations, even those that are legal issues.

I Think I Can, I Think I Can . . .

It's easy to get bogged down in feeling like you *canít* do anything. That's how you end up being a whipped parent. Take a careful look at the two following examples. The only thing that *canít* be done is to *make* an adolescent meet a hope or expectation: you can't physically force your child to go to school. You *canít* physically control your child's behavior. Now look at all the *can* statements. It turns out there are many more things you *can* do, than not. But being unable to control Jack's behavior makes it feel like it's the other way around.

Using the TOES model, you may decide you need to put more effort into your part of providing opportunities. If so, list your plans for each step, using the blank form in Appendix A (page 151). Write down as many *can* statements as possible, and put them into action. *It will help you feel more powerful and in control of yourself.* You can then feel assured that you are providing your child with every opportunity possible to meet your hope or expectation. He may not choose to take advantage of those opportunities, but you will have done all you *can* do as a parent.

Staying On Your TOES

Example One: Hopes

Society expects and I hope that my child will go to school. But, I canít physically force him to go. I can stay on my TOES.

Tell him I hope he goes to school.

Opportunities are presented for him to meet my hope:

- I *can* register him at the school.
- I *can* buy him an alarm clock and give him two wake up calls in the morning.
- I *can* provide him with school supplies he may need.
- I *can* make sure he has a way of getting to and from school. (This does not include driving him if he refuses to get out of bed and misses the bus.)

Educate him with knowledge to help him choose whether or not he's going to try to meet my hope:

- I *can* tell him I believe it's hard to get a job without a diploma.
- I *can* tell him that others are often critical of people who have quit school.
- I *can* let him know that if he doesn't go to school he may end up in court or on probation, because truancy is illegal.
- I *can* tell him that I am going to protect myself from educational neglect charges by calling the school every morning that he refuses to go, and letting them know I've done my part in getting him to school. I'll tell them this is not an excused absence. I'll keep a personal calendar where I write down dates and the names of those to whom I've spoken.

Show (or model) it.

- I *can* go back to school and get my diploma or GED.
- I *can* read the newspaper or books.

Staying On Your TOES

Example Two: Expectations

I can expect that my adolescent will not become violent toward me or anyone else in my home, and I know I canít physically control my adolescentís behavior. I can stay on my TOES.

Tell him I expect him to handle things without becoming violent.

Opportunities are presented for him to meet my expectation:

- I *can* choose not to escalate any intense situations when my child is angry.
- I *can* provide a cooling-off area where my child can go when he's angry.
- I *can* allow him to leave the room or house, if he needs to, so that he may calm down before getting violent. I can stop myself from following him.
- I *can* allow him to vent his anger with words instead of physical aggression, without interrupting or getting into a screaming match.

Educate him with knowledge to help him choose whether or not he's going to try to meet my expectation:

- I *can* tell him physical aggression toward someone is illegal. It's considered assault.
- I *can* tell him how I will respond to physical violence against myself or anyone in my home — I will call the police. (We'll talk more about this in Chapter Seventeen on working with agencies, like the court and police).

Show (or model) it.

- I *can* never be physically violent or aggressive toward anyone else, including my adolescent.
- I *can* calmly handle conflicts with others, including my adolescent.
- I *can* leave the room or take a personal "time out" before my own anger gets out of control.

Chapter Seven

Carol Brady Never Lived with Jack

It is just as important to have realistic expectations for yourself, as a parent, as you do for your adolescent. Remember, expectations are dangerous, and, as you have learned, they set you up for disappointment. You came to have expectations for yourself the same way you did for Jack —

When You Wish Upon a Star . . .

Think back to when you first discovered you were going to be a parent. What hopes did you have for yourself? What picture did you paint of yourself as a mother or father? Did you imagine you would always be patient, loving and effective as a parent? It probably never occurred to you that a day might come when you wouldn't feel kindly toward your child. Your picture didn't include looking forward to the day he moves out of your home. After all, *good* parents aren't supposed to think like that, right?

Your hopes and dreams for yourself as a parent may have developed before your child was even conceived — especially if you waited until later in life to have a child. You had plenty of time to imagine what you would be like as a parent. It may have started as early as your own childhood, when you played "house." Did you ever play a mommy who screamed at her baby doll and threw it down in frustration because it wouldn't do what you wanted? Probably not. You played a parent who took care of that baby, nurtured, cuddled and loved it. Those first dreams started right then. The problem is that the baby doll never grew up and acted like Jack.

Iíll Never Be Like My Mother (or Father)

Another way that we form expectations for ourselves is based on what our own parents were like. Many of us vow we will be *better* than our own parents: "I'll never yell at or hit my kids the way my mother did to me" or "I'll spend more time with my son than my dad did with me" or "I'll never lose my temper with my child, the way my parents did with me."

The flip side of the coin is when you feel you had *good* parents and vow you will be just as *good* with your own child: "My parents never physically disciplined me, and I'm not going to do that with my kids either" or "My mom gave me almost everything I ever needed, and I'm going to do the same for my child."

The problem with that coin (both sides), is that you are not your parent, and you're raising Jack. Seems obvious doesn't it? But it's easy to fall into the trap of comparing yourself to your own parents. If you've formed expectations — for yourself — based on your own parents, you've set yourself up for disappointment.

> *Youíre a different person,*
> *Jackís a different kid,*
> *and this is a new era.*

What Kind of a Parent
Will Other People Think I Am?

Society doesn't just have expectations for Jack. There are all sorts of expectations for you, too. Again, society often makes these expectations clear through laws. You are expected to provide your child with food, shelter and clothing. You are expected to discipline your child without leaving physical signs of abuse. If you don't meet those expectations, Protective Services may take your child and throw you in jail.

Society also communicates informal expectations. You know what they are. When your child throws a fit in a store or restaurant, everyone looks at you, clearly communicating, "Get that kid under control." When your adolescent acts out at school, the teacher calls you and lets you know, "We expect you to get your child's behavior under control."

The expectations society places on parents are often unrealistic. As parents, we usually internalize those expectations and make them our own. When we fail to live up to those expectations, we may feel ashamed, bitter and guilty. Those emotions make it even tougher to respond to Jack calmly and effectively.

Generational Expectations

Expectations handed down throughout generations of your family don't affect the expectations you have for just your child. They also affect the expectations you have for yourself, as a parent. Ms. Booker says, "My mother tells me all the time that I need to control Brandy. She says I should be doing a better job with my daughter. That really burns me. At the same time, I can't help but think she's right."

A good way to tell if someone has an expectation of you as a parent is if you hear the words *need*, *ought* or *should*. Should is a really bad word. It can leave a person feeling inadequate, embarrassed and guilty. It means someone is judging you (or in this case, your parenting skills), according to their own life experiences. Family members are famous for this — well-intentioned or not.

It's the rare individual who can say, "Yup, my parents think I'm doing a great job raising Jack (or even Jill)." That's because every generation has expectations for the next. Those expectations are usually unrealistic and are rooted in the idea that you can control your child. Your family is bound to have an opinion on your parenting skills. If it's a critical one, you're in good company.

Realistic Expectations

Finding middle ground for yourself as a parent means no longer beating yourself up emotionally for unmet expectations that were unrealistic to begin with. It also means recognizing what you *can* do as a parent. The only thing you can do is stay on your TOES. If you find yourself forgetting what that means, go back to Chapter Six (page 53) again and reread it.

ìWard, the Beaver just got arrested for shoplifting.î

June Cleaver and Carol Brady rarely fell short of the expectations society held for them, or even those they held for themselves. That's because their children (in the wonderful world of television) were Beaver, Greg and Marcia. You're not raising any of those kids. You live with Jack. Let's face it, if Marcia had come home and said she was dating Jack, Mr. Brady may have been driven to get out his Daisy Red Ryder Western Carbine air rifle.

Until you accept that your child's personality is not going to change, you will continue to have unrealistic expectations for yourself, and of him. You will continue to wake up every morning with the hope that he's going to transform into Greg or Beaver (or even Wally). It's not going to happen. Your adolescent's personality is just the way it is . . . there's nothing waiting behind door number two. Once you accept him for who he is, you'll be able to get past the expectations and feelings that are leaving you feeling whipped.

CHAPTER EIGHT

Feelings

When we first began using the CRAP method with parents, the message we got was, "It's not really helpful to talk about our feelings. We want more information on what consequences will work."

Ready, Set, Go!

There are two main reasons parents want to focus on consequences for their teen without working on their own feelings. First, you may want to get right to consequences because it feels like you're *doing* something constructive. When you're feeling anxious, you want a plan. You want to take action. Part of that goes back to the issue of control. What can I do? What can I control? Second, talking about the feelings Jack brings out in you is probably *uncomfortable*. Why? Because it's all about *you*. It means recognizing how your own feelings and emotional needs affect your parenting approach.

We said in the beginning that our goal is not to help you figure out how to control or change your adolescent. Our goal is to help you figure out how you can change *yourself,* in ways that may or may not impact your adolescent. We can't say that enough. You're now at Chapter Eight. If you're still trying to figure out how to control Jack through consequences, and if you think your own emotions are "nice to talk about but not really that important," you need to do one of two things: change your way of thinking or throw this book away.

Getting to the Heart of It

Your emotions are the bottom line — literally. If you want to move up from the bottom, you've got to work on your feelings. Even if it's uncomfortable. Even if it's petrifying. Consequences are very important, and we will get to them in Chapter Eleven. (You may have even flipped to that chapter as soon as you bought this book, before reading anything else.) People often feel better knowing there's something they can *do*. But how you handle your emotions is at the heart of what you can control.

Before we dive into those unpleasant feelings, we need to recognize that you do experience *some* pleasant emotions in relation to your adolescent. Think of a pleasant feeling you've had toward your child recently: a moment that touched your heart, an incident that was funny, a feeling of happiness or love. (Happiness that your kid has left the room doesn't count.) If you can't think of any pleasant emotion you've felt toward your child after five minutes, then make a conscious effort this week to pay special attention to any enjoyable feeling toward your child. Write it down to remind yourself that there *are* those feelings to be experienced. When you live with a teenager like Jack, it's easy to get caught up in all the negative feelings that come along. Don't let the positive feelings go by without noticing them.

Tackling Unpleasant Emotions

Now let's tackle those unpleasant emotions that go hand-in-hand with parenting Jack. You can't completely control what emotions you have. If that were possible, no one would ever experience anger, sadness, unhappiness or fear. However, there are two things you can control: your *awareness* of your emotions and how you *respond* to them.

Each of us has emotional buttons that can be pushed at any time.

Your adolescent knows you very well — maybe better than anyone. He knows exactly how to push those buttons to get a reaction out of you. Sometimes he may push your buttons without even meaning to do so.

Pushing your emotional buttons is the biggest advantage Jack has over you. If he can get you off track by targeting an unpleasant feeling (hurt, anger, disappointment, embarrassment) he accomplishes his goal. The focus is taken off his behavior, and it's redirected to your emotions. When you're emotional, it muddies up the water. It also gives Jack a sense of power. Think about it. You know that if you can really upset someone or get a reaction, you've got a lot of control over that situation. If you can become more *aware* of your emotional "weak spots," you can strengthen your ability to rationally *respond* to your adolescent. You'll be able to stay calm and avoid getting off track. You'll keep some control over your emotions.

Mrs. Whippet's weak spots were guilt and anger, and Slug knew it. Brandy loved to push Ms. Booker's anger button. Top Dog's mom was sick from the fear and guilt she constantly experienced. The emotions you experience most with your adolescent will depend on your personality, life experiences and insecurities. If you can figure out what your own emotional buttons are, you'll be more prepared. You'll be able to recognize the words or behavior Jack uses to try and push those buttons. You'll be able to control how you respond. Your emotions do *not* have to dominate the way you react to your child.

Anger

Anger is a common feeling named by the parents with whom we've worked. Anger about an adolescent's disrespect and bad attitude. Anger that one's property has been destroyed. Anger that one's personal and work life is disrupted because of Jack's behavior. Anger that a child doesn't appreciate all of the time, money and energy spent on him. Most of all, anger related to feeling a loss of control.

Anger typically masks other emotions, ones that can leave you more vulnerable. It may be safer to admit being angry than being sad, scared, embarrassed or disappointed. "I was furious when Jack was arrested for shoplifting." Yes, you probably were. But what else were you feeling? Since the emotions may be fleeting before they turn to anger, it will take an inner-search to grasp those initial feelings.

One reason it's so important to identify your emotions *before* they turn to anger is because parents often respond in anger to an adolescent's bad behavior. If you're not aware of your emotional buttons and weak spots, you're more likely to react in anger. That can lead to guilt and shame. Have you ever yelled at, shamed or hit your child in anger? How did you feel afterward? When the anger passes, you may be left with emotions related to your angry reaction, like shame and guilt, which leave you more whipped than ever. You must become *aware* of your emotions before you can control how you *respond* to them.

Brandy's mother identified anger as the most intense feeling she experienced toward her daughter. In anger, she often called her daughter names and escalated arguments with Brandy. Ms. Booker also set up Brandy sometimes, hoping that Brandy would get in trouble with the law. Afterward, Ms. Booker felt ashamed and guilty. She felt terrible about the things she had done to Brandy. She wished she had handled her anger differently. "Everything I do seems to leave me feeling worse," she admitted. That's because Ms. Booker was responding out of emotion, with little thought about how she might feel afterward.

Frustration

Closely related to anger is frustration. Frustration is a feeling that all parents experience at one time or another. Parents who have adolescents like Jack will feel its presence quite often. Frustration develops when you feel a loss of control over any situation. There's something you want to happen, and you're powerless to make it occur. Your son is using marijuana and alcohol, you want him to stop, he won't, and you can't *make* him stop. Your daughter has a habit of swearing at you, has run away several times, and refuses to do even one chore around the house. You want her behavior to change, but no matter what you say or do, she continues to make the same choices. When you feel powerless because you can't control someone or something, you become frustrated and, ultimately, whipped.

Remember, you have little control, if any, over your adolescent's behavior unless he decides to *let you* have some control. If your goal is to regain power and authority over a kid like Jack, give it up. You probably never had it to begin with. If you continue to try and *make* your teen behave the way you think he should, you'll be frustrated for a *very* long time to come.

The good news is that you can control one very important thing: yourself. You can control how you respond to your adolescent and his behaviors. Start by becoming more aware of those times when you're feeling frustrated. Figure out what helps you cope with feelings of frustration. Talking to a friend? Finding humor in the situation? Taking time for yourself to meditate or do something you enjoy? See Chapter Eighteen for suggestions on ways to nurture yourself. Don't try to escape your emotions with alcohol, drugs or avoidance.

Remember, no matter how hard you try, *you can't control another person's behavior.* You can change only your own behavior and hope it has an impact on your child's choices. Keep in mind, you can only *hope*, and if this hope turns into an *expectation* . . . well, you know the risk involved.

Worry

Another emotion every parent experiences is worry. Worry is rooted in fear. Parents we've worked with whose adolescents are risk-takers or have severe behavior problems shared some of these worries:

- "I worry he'll end up behind bars, *or in them.*"
- "I worry she'll get hurt or even die."
- "I worry he'll end up hurting or even killing someone else."
- "I worry she'll end up pregnant or with AIDS."

As parents, we have some control over our worries and fears when our children are young. We can take steps, or actions, to lessen our worries. There's something we can *do* to help protect a child. For instance, we may worry about our child's health and thus take him in for regular checkups with a pediatrician. We may worry about his safety and take steps to lessen the likelihood of accidents by "childproofing" the home, holding his hand when crossing the road and waiting with him at the bus stop. We can control who babysits for him. If there's someone we don't know or trust, we can make sure our child is never left alone with that person. The older a child gets, the less control a parent has over his behavior. Control that, in the past, lessened worries. There are fewer things we can *do*. This is especially true once a child hits adolescence.

Parents typically worry excessively about their children. We worry about them using drugs or alcohol, or getting in with "the wrong crowd." We worry about their education, or that they aren't living up to their full potential. We worry about them having accidents, ones we cannot take steps to prevent. We can no longer hold his hand when he crosses the road. *He* now has control over who he gets into a car, or is alone, with. This feeling of loss of control can exaggerate a parent's worries into full-blown anxiety.

Worry creates heavy burdens for parents. How can you live a happy, relaxed life when you are often preoccupied, sometimes overwhelmed, with fears about things that are out of your control? Worry also creates a burden for adolescents. It's good for a child to know you care and are concerned for his well-being. It's disturbing for an adolescent to know you are so worried about him that you are sick and have trouble sleeping at night. How would you feel if one of your parents let you know they are so worried about you that it makes them sick? You probably wouldn't feel too secure about yourself.

Top Dog's mother identified worry as the emotion she felt the strongest and most often. She said the constant worry she had that something tragic would happen to her son had caused her to become physically ill. She developed an ulcer and got migraine headaches. She often had panic attacks without warning. She wondered if worrying so much would take years off her life. She needed to find a way to get rid of that big, ugly monster, known as worry, so she could start enjoying her life again.

Think about the fears or worries you have in life, outside of your child's behaviors. Finances? Marital problems? Health of a relative or friend? Work? How do you normally cope with such concerns? Is it similar to or different from how you cope with worry related to your adolescent? You may need to strengthen your coping skills, in general.

There are several excellent books regarding relaxation and coping skills, available at your local library or bookstore. We have provided a recommended reading list (page 163), should you want more help in this area. You may also want to see a therapist for some ideas on ways to handle anxiety.

First and foremost, however, is accepting that you cannot control your adolescent's choices or be there twenty-four hours a day to hold his hand. Accepting this can help lessen the anxiety you feel. Your adolescent will make choices, good and bad, every day for the rest of his life. In fact, he has been doing *just that* for quite some time, whether you've realized it or not. He will continue to do so, with or without you, and whether you worry or not.

Sometimes being preoccupied with concerns for your child means you are spending too much time focusing on your child, and not enough time focusing on your own life. One parent we worked with made the comment, "I was put on this Earth to worry about my child." Wrong! Has your adolescent ever told you to "get a life?" What he's telling you is, "Quit being so wrapped up in me." Consider how much mental energy you use when you worry. Worrying is a waste of time. Think of all the things you can do with that energy other than using it up on worry. You can continue to spend most of your time focused on your adolescent and the fact that you have little control over his choices. Or you can fill the worry space with other things that will nurture and reacquaint you with yourself, in roles other than "mother" or "father." We'll explore this more in Chapter Eighteen, "Nurturing Yourself."

Guilt

Some parents find themselves spending hours reviewing all the things they have ever done *wrong* to their child. At any given moment, Ms. Booker could pull up her mental list of "mistakes" she'd made with Brandy. It went something like this:

"I let my daughter cry sometimes when she was a baby."

"I spent too much time away from her when she was little because I had to work."

"I divorced her father when Brandy was six years old. That really messed her up."

"She hated my boyfriend when she was seven years old. But I was selfish and wouldn't break up with him."

"I used to get frustrated too easily. I yelled at her too much."

"I told my daughter I hated her. I've never forgiven myself for that."

Creating a mental list of all your wrongdoings as a parent is very common when you have a child like Jack (or even if you have a kid like Jill). These parents are searching for an answer to the ever-popular question,

¿Why is my kid acting like this? Is it something I did?¿

Remember our philosophy? Your child has his own personality, his own brain and he is choosing how he *wants to be.* "Good" kids can come from bad homes and environments. "Bad" kids can come from good homes and environments. We could give many examples of kids who have risen above bad situations, just like this one:

Candy is sixteen years old. She was raised in a crack house. She doesn't know who her father is, and her mother is a crack-cocaine addict. Candy remembers spending many of her younger years being hungry. Once in a while, when her mother was sober enough, they would walk to the soup kitchen to get a free meal.

When she became a teenager, Candy decided she needed to talk to someone about her life. She got on the bus, went to a mental health agency and asked if she could see a therapist. She never missed an appointment during the year she was in therapy. In spite of a terribly difficult childhood, in which the odds were certainly against her, she is turning herself into a successful individual. She attends school during the day and works part-time in the afternoon and on weekends. She is saving money so she can eventually get her own place to live.

Candy has expectations of herself that include going to college, having a professional career and someday living in a nice home with a husband and children. She's taking steps to accomplish those goals. Born with a personality and mind that will take her where she wants to go, Candy is a survivor.

History is filled with stories of people who have accomplished great things, despite great odds against them and without the guidance, hopes and expectations of a caring parent. Today, thousands of "Candys" are successful and happy because they found strength and determination within themselves. Yes, environment, background, parenting and a hundred other factors affect the course of a life. Adolf Hitler's mother probably had a different approach to parenting than Mahatma Gandhi's mother. But it's important to recognize that, ultimately, everyone makes their own choices. The final responsibility lies with the individual — not his friends, teachers or parents.

Each of us makes mistakes. If we learn from those mistakes, we grow. When you find yourself running through your *guilt list*, think about what you learned from each situation. Would you handle the same situation differently now? If you feel guilty for calling your child names or hitting him, stop now. Do things differently, starting today. Every parent has things they wish they had done differently. Yes, you probably did make some mistakes. You'll probably continue to make mistakes. The important thing is to learn from them and stop repeating them.

Feeling guilty is like serving a prison sentence. With each item on your mental list, ask yourself: *how long should I punish myself for that mistake?* How long is a fair sentence? A week? A month? A year? Some parents spend longer than that agonizing over where they *went wrong* with Jack. If you're still carrying around guilt from mistakes made long ago, set yourself free now. Time served. Forgive yourself. Apologize to your child, if it will make you feel better. Then choose the things you want to start doing differently with your child, so you won't fall back into the same guilt trap. Even if Jack continues to have behavior problems, how you choose to respond to him will determine whether you go to bed tonight feeling guilty or good about yourself.

Top Dog's mother truly believed she had control over his choice to use drugs and alcohol. She believed there had to be *something* she could do to get him to stop fighting. Because of those beliefs, she experienced tremendous guilt (not to mention lots of other unpleasant emotions). She mentally tortured herself with guilt on a daily basis. She would flip through her Rolodex of wrongdoings and blame herself for his problems:

> "I should have known my son would have a problem with drugs. His father was an alcoholic. I never should have had a baby with him. If I had chosen someone else, Top Dog wouldn't have this gene that's destroying his life."

She also had a list of all the things she *could have* tried in order to change her son's behavior, but didn't:

> "I should have sent him to counseling when he was twelve-years-old and I first found out he was smoking pot. I just thought it was a phase. If I'd tried to get him help sooner, he might not have gotten addicted."

Top Dog's mom didn't just have a carry-on bag of guilt, she had the complete luggage set. For her to dump some of that baggage, she had to accept that Top Dog has the ultimate control and responsibility for his own behavior. In fact, drug and alcohol addicts routinely feed into someone else's guilt about their substance abuse. As soon as *anyone* tries to take responsibility for another person's addiction, the addict will jump on the opportunity to shift the blame. This is also common with kids like Jack:

> "I'm not responsible for my behavior — you are."

> "I ran away because you were being such a bitch to me."

> "I stole those jeans because you never buy me any clothes."

(Basically, "I know I did it, but it's your fault.")

Top Dog's mom had to realize that she was not responsible for her son's behavior. Once she accepted that, she was able to move on. She attended her Al-Anon meetings for regular support and felt less burdened with worry and guilt. Now she's in a position to enjoy her own life. Sure, she still worries sometimes. And sometimes she packs her bag and takes a guilt trip. But now it's only a carry-on bag. She knows Top Dog will change only if he decides it's something *he* wants to do.

Hurt

Parents who feel hurt by their child's behavior are often left feeling extremely vulnerable. You may even start to put up emotional "walls" to keep from getting too close to your adolescent, for fear you'll be hurt again. Ms. Booker once said, "The only time Brandy wants to have anything to do with me is if she wants something. I'm not even going to give her the chance to hurt me again. That may sound cold, but it's how I feel."

Like many parents, Ms. Booker needed to find an emotional middle ground. It is extreme behavior to remain distant from your child. (Not only is that unhealthy, it's almost impossible to do.) The other extreme is taking your adolescent's choices and behavior personally, so that your feelings are constantly hurt. Hurt feelings develop when you take someone else's behavior *personally*, which means believing that the behavior has something to do with you. We'll look at personalizing more in Chapter Thirteen. It's at the core of feeling hurt. It's also at the heart of disappointment.

It's hard not to take some of Jack's behavior personally. When someone (especially your child) calls you a name, destroys your things or continually breaks the law, leaving you to pay thousands of dollars in court costs, it feels *personal*. On top of that, the emotional needs that played a part in your decision to have and raise Jack aren't being met. That may also hurt. However, your child is *not* responsible for your emotional well-being. You are the only one responsible for your own emotional state.

You may feel sad for your child when you see him making choices that you believe are destructive. But if you've stayed on your TOES, sad is as far as it should go. There's a big difference between feeling sad and being hurt about your adolescent's behavior. Sad is okay. Hurt will leave you whipped.

Acceptance

Your feelings are related to how much you accept your child for who he is. The more you believe you need to change Jack, the more unpleasant emotions (like guilt, anger, frustration, and disappointment) you will experience. Accepting your child doesn't mean that you agree with all of his choices. It does mean that you accept his personality, faults and all. If you keep trying to turn him into Greg Brady or Beaver Cleaver, you'll never accept him for who he is: Jack. You'll continue to experience feelings that leave you whipped.

Now that you've explored your feelings and know which ones are causing you the most pain and grief, you're ready to move on to the next chapter. We're going to help you learn to cope, and even change, some of your negative feelings into positive or neutral ones. You really are going to feel better.

CHAPTER NINE

The Thunderstorm

When you're a whipped parent, negative emotions weigh you down. This chapter will show you a trick that will help you get rid of some of those negative emotions. You will feel lighter and be able to stand tall again.

Itís a Bird, Itís a Plane . . . What the Heck Is That?

Feelings don't come out of nowhere. It may seem like it sometimes, but they don't. Your feelings are rooted in your thoughts. It's that simple. If you can change your thoughts about a situation, you will change the way you feel. You may not get rid of those unpleasant emotions entirely (that would be really hard to do); however, you may be able to lessen them. When you change your thoughts, your feelings will be different, and you will behave differently. Your actions will be much different if you are feeling happy, secure or confident rather than feeling scared, angry or hurt.

The problem is that thoughts and feelings aren't visible. You can't see them. I don't know what you're thinking or feeling. I can make guesses based on the one thing I *can* see — your behavior. If you're crying, I may guess that you're sad. If you're yelling, I may guess that you're angry. I may or may not be right. I can also make guesses about what you're thinking, based on your actions. Again, I may be right or wrong. Unless you come right out and tell me your thoughts, I'll just be mind-reading. And mind-reading is dangerous to everyone involved.

The Thunderstorm Model

Thoughts, feelings and actions are a package deal. This package is like a thunderstorm. A person's action is like lightning: you see it. Thoughts and feelings are like the cloud conditions in the sky, above the lightning. It's impossible to see what's going on in those clouds. You can only guess, based on the lightning.

An adolescent who fights with peers is an example of seeing lightning, without knowing the conditions leading up to the behavior. Adolescents get into physical fights for all sorts of reasons. Sometimes it truly is because the kid is angry and becomes aggressive. He may react impulsively, without thinking it through. But it's a mistake to believe this is the only reason teenagers fight. Today's adolescents live in a culture of violence. It's in their music, their schools, their homes and their gangs. Many live in neighborhoods or attend schools where to fight is to survive. Yes, they *have* thought it through. No, going to a teacher or walking away may *not* be an option. In some places, to do so is seen as a sign of weakness and may end up being more dangerous than fighting. The point is, you see the fighting, but you don't necessarily know what's behind it.

Target's dad doesn't understand why his son continues to get into fights at school. Target is on probation for shoplifting and truancy. Every time he assaults a peer, he gets sent to detention. He's been in therapy for almost a year to find alternatives to fighting with no apparent success. His father, therapist and probation officer came to conclude that Target must actually *like* the excitement of fighting.

What no one stopped to consider was that Target goes to school with some very dangerous peers. He *thinks* that, if he doesn't fight, he'll be seen as weak and targeted by those peers, who have access to all sorts of weapons. He *feels* scared, and this fear leads to other feelings of vulnerability and shame. He responds to these *thoughts and feelings* with the *actions* of getting into physical fights. Target *thinks* that if he fights, other kids will see him as tough and leave him alone. This makes him *feel* less frightened, more secure and confident. Consequences he may suffer at home, school or detention aren't as important to him as how he's viewed by his peers. After all, to him it is survival. He continues to *act* in a way that adults in his life don't understand. Sometimes he doesn't even understand his behavior himself, because he's not always aware of his thoughts and feelings.

Top Dog is another adolescent who fights on a regular basis. His mother sees his *actions*, and mind-reads the thoughts and feelings behind them. She believes that her son fights out of anger. "His dad left us when Top Dog was seven, and he's never gotten over it. When his dad was around, he used to hit both of us, and I think my son learned to use violence as a way to handle things." Top Dog's mom has taken him to several therapists, trying to help him resolve his "anger problem," but he continues to fight. That's because Top Dog isn't angry. He isn't thinking about his dad. Top Dog is a risk-taker. Top Dog *thinks* he's cool. He *thinks* he's tough. This leaves him *feeling* excited and pumped up, which gives him an adrenaline rush. He responds to these *thoughts and feelings* by *acting*: he gets into fights. Top Dog is an athlete, and his sport is street-fighting. He prides himself on being very good at it. After winning a fight, Top Dog *thinks* he's tough and bad, and *feels* confident and smug. So, he continues to *act* in a way that keeps him living on the edge of danger while also feeling like the king of the hill.

In both cases, the only thing visible to others was the behavior of these two young men: fighting. Thoughts and feelings that led to the behavior weren't visible. Target and Top Dog had very different reasons behind their actions. The adults in their lives recognized the lightning, but were wrong when they guessed about the clouds.

Using the Thunderstorm Model

The other problem with thoughts and feelings is that it's extremely tough to uncover them. When you find yourself acting or doing something (like screaming at your kid), it's hard to figure out the thoughts and feelings that led you to act that way. Remember the last chapter, and how complicated feelings are? Recognizing your thoughts is even more complicated. You may get some of the obvious ones immediately: "When I screamed at my son, I was thinking he was being disrespectful and mean. I felt angry." If you keep digging, there are probably many more thoughts and feelings you aren't conscious of: "When I screamed at my son, I was thinking I must have done something wrong as a parent for him to act like this. I was feeling disappointed and guilty."

Mrs. Whippet often found herself reacting to her son in ways she didn't understand and definitely didn't like. "Every little thing he does irritates me. He was talking to his girlfriend in the rudest, meanest way the other day. I just flew off the handle and told him he didn't deserve a girlfriend. Of course, he told me it wasn't any of my business, which really made me mad. I ended up chasing him around the kitchen table, screaming at him. Can you imagine? I can't believe I did that. I don't know what came over me."

The only thing visible in that situation was Mrs. Whippet's *action*: chasing her son around the table. She felt that behavior came "out of nowhere." It didn't. She had to do some digging to find out where it did come from.

Using the thunderstorm model, Mrs. Whippet worked her way back from the lightning, her *action*. The first and most obvious *feeling* she identified was anger. Then she remembered that anger often masks other feelings. So she dug deeper and realized she'd felt scared. That made no sense to her: "Why would I be scared? Or even mad, for that matter? He wasn't being rude to me. He was being rude to his girlfriend. It just irritated the heck out of me." The anger came so rapidly after the feeling of fear that she hadn't even been aware of it.

Recognizing that this incident was just one of the many times she found herself "irritated" with Slug, Mrs. Whippet continued working her way up the thunderstorm model. She began paying attention to the *thoughts* she had right before she got irritated. What she discovered was that when she got irritated by "little things," the thought that usually popped into her mind was, "Oh my God, that's just like his father." Slug's *biological* father — not Mr. Whippet.

Identifying her thoughts helped Mrs. Whippet realize that her actions did *not* come out of nowhere. When Slug was mean to his girlfriend, Mrs. Whippet *thought* it was just like his biological father had treated her. When Slug pierced his ear, grew his hair longer than she wanted, or simply walked into the room she *thought*, "He looks just like his father." This led her to *feel* scared, because she *thinks* Slug's father is a "loser." She also *feels* angry when she thinks of his father. She then ends up irritated with her son. These *thoughts and feelings* caused Mrs. Whippet to *act* in a way that she regretted: yelling, criticizing or chasing her son around the table.

The thoughts Mrs. Whippet had of Slug's father were so fleeting, she had to dig hard to become aware of them. Once she found this awareness, she realized her thoughts and feelings were at the heart of how she acted toward her son. She was able to change her thoughts. She replaced, "Oh, God, he looks like his father" with "My son is a handsome young man." When Slug was rude to his girlfriend, she replaced, "He's going to turn out just like his father," with "This isn't my relationship. My relationship with my husband is respectful, and all we can do is model that for Slug. It's up to him how he handles things with his girlfriend." Another thought she began using was, "All I'm seeing are his actions. I don't know the whole story. I don't know what he's thinking or feeling."

Changing Thoughts

Changing Mrs. Whippet's thoughts wasn't easy; it took a great deal of practice. Being aware of her thoughts was the first step. By changing her thoughts, and thus her feelings, she was able to change her actions. Instead of chasing or criticizing her son, she was able to give him space. She was able to wait until he was calm, and return later to ask him, "Is everything okay? You seemed upset earlier. Would you like to talk?" Sometimes Slug took her up on the offer; often he didn't. Most importantly, Mrs. Whippet *felt* better, and no longer *acted* in ways that she regretted.

Top Dog's mom credits learning to change her thoughts with saving her life. A year ago, if her son had told her he was going out with friends, her immediate thought was, "Oh no. He'll probably get drunk and start a fight." She would picture him facing a gang, all carrying tire irons and guns. She *thought* Top Dog would end up a bloody mess. These *thoughts* left her *feeling* fear for her son's life. She *thought* her son's life was in danger every time he went out. These *thoughts and feelings* made her sick, and they showed in her *actions*. She would sag to the couch, ill-faced and fatigued. She would say to her son, "Why do you always put me through this hell? You know I don't want you going out tonight."

One of the things that helped Top Dog's mom regain her emotional well-being was practicing how to change her thoughts so her feelings wouldn't leave her whipped. When she encountered a situation that made her sick, she sat and wrote down all the thoughts and feelings she experienced. She dug deeply to reach the ones that were hidden. Then she made a list of thoughts she could use to replace the ones that left her feeling whipped. She did this every time she found herself thinking or feeling things she didn't like. And it worked.

To change your actions, you need to change your feelings.

You cannot change your feelings until you change your thoughts.

Thoughts can be changed.

Here's an example of how Top Dog's mom changed a few of her negative, hair-raising thoughts. Working backward from her actions (lightning), she was able to uncover her feelings and thoughts:

Action — She was begging, bribing and crying. *(Why? What was she feeling?)*

Feelings — She was scared, hurt and disappointed. *(Why? What thoughts made her feel this way?)*

Thoughts — She was thinking her son might get killed. That he didn't care about her. That he might end up in prison. That he could be seriously injured.

Once Top Dog's mother identified the thoughts that were leaving her feeling whipped, she started working to change her negative thoughts to ones that would help her feel more comfortable:

New Thoughts ó Top Dog knows what he's doing out there in the world. I have faith that he will do what makes *him* happy. I'll remind myself that it's his life, not mine.

New Feelings ó Confident that Top dog will take care of himself. Less scared and worried.

New Actions ó She is calmer.

Staying on Your TOES

Another positive thought Top Dog's mom uses is, *I stay on my TOES:*

- "I **T**ell him my hopes."

- "**O**pportunities are provided for him to seek help." (See a therapist or get substance abuse treatment.)

- "I **E**ducate him on the dangers and legalities of his actions."

- "I **S**how him by modeling. I don't drink, use drugs or fight."

This helps ease her guilt. She knows she's done all she can. She feels better and she sleeps better.

Change a Thought ó Change a Life

One parent said she changed her entire life by changing just one thought. Every time her child came into the room she would think, *Here comes the demon spawn from hell.*

This thought left her feeling disgusted, angry and hateful. She replaced that negative thought with, *Here comes my confused angel-child from God.* It took her a little time, but eventually she began to actually feel love and concern for her child.

The next time you find yourself feeling bad, having negative thoughts, or acting in ways you don't like, sit down and make your list. Divide it into three sections: Negative Actions, Negative Feelings, Negative Thoughts. After you have your list completed, focus on the section of negative thoughts. For each negative thought write down a positive — or at least a neutral thought — that you can replace it with. Use the form provided in Appendix B (page 155).

Examining Behavior

Now that you're thinking more positively, we're going to take an honest, realistic look at your teen's behavior. The next chapter focuses on determining which of your child's behaviors are truly serious, simply annoying, or somewhere in between.

CHAPTER TEN

Behavior

*N*ow you have a new way of looking at your child's behavior: it's only the lightning that you're able to see. It can be caused by any number of things, most of which are hidden in the clouds. You know that you can change your reaction to your adolescent's behavior by changing your thoughts. Sometimes letting him get things off his chest is all you need to do. Sometimes he just needs the opportunity to think things through on his own. But other times, he needs to experience consequences. So how do you know which of Jack's behaviors need consequences and which you can let slide for now?

Triaging Behaviors

Deciding which behaviors are tolerable or truly intolerable isn't easy. In a perfect world, *all* of Jack's negative behaviors would be intolerable. In the real world, there's no way to give consequences for every behavior you feel is a problem. You'd probably be giving out consequences all day long. You would stay whipped, simply from exhaustion. Besides, when an adolescent is "called on" every negative thing he does, he becomes whipped himself. It's exhausting to have someone point out everything you do wrong. It's nagging, and it may even provoke him to behave worse.

The first thing you can do is start thinking about your child's negative behaviors in three ways: mild, moderate and severe. You are the only one who can decide which behaviors you can or can't live with in your home. Write down the behaviors that concern you most about your child. Your list will depend on what you've determined are realistic expectations for your adolescent (see Chapter Five, page 45). Ms. Booker's list looked very different than Mrs. Whippet's. Top Dog's mom had a list different than both of theirs.

Severe Behaviors include legal and safety issues. Shoplifting, truancy, assault and drug use would all fit in this category. Destruction of your property or home and taking your car without permission could also be considered severe behaviors. Mrs. Whippet decided that Slug's refusal to attend school was a severe behavior, because it affected her in a way that she wouldn't tolerate. Ms. Booker listed Brandy's severe behaviors as hitting, shoving and sneaking out of the house. She also felt staying out past city curfew was severe, because she (as a parent) could be held responsible for Brandy's behavior. Top Dog's mom felt his use of drugs and alcohol was severe. She also decided his decision to fight was a severe behavior.

Mild Behaviors are irritating and unpleasant, but you can live with them if you have to. Messy rooms, complaining about chores (but eventually doing them), slamming doors and stomping out of the room in anger are very typical of adolescence. So is being on the phone constantly, whining, arguing and swearing (without directing it at you). Mrs. Whippet decided that having to constantly remind Slug to do his chores and clean his messy room were mild when compared to his refusal to go to school. Ms. Booker figured that Brandy's habits of swearing at her and being "disrespectful" were mild when compared to her tendency to get violent and stay out late. Top Dog's mom figured anything other than fighting and using drugs were mild behaviors for her son.

Moderate Behaviors are somewhere in between mild and severe. Some of these may be constant profanity (often directed toward you), refusing to do any chores and occasionally breaking curfew. Moderate behaviors may feel intolerable, but are still of less concern than severe behaviors. Mrs. Whippet decided that Slug's profanity was a moderate concern. Ms. Booker, on the other hand, was experiencing more severe problems with her daughter than Mrs. Whippet was with Slug. Ms. Booker saw profanity in her home as mild. However, she felt Brandy's outright refusal to do *anything* to help around the house moderately concerned her. Top Dog's mom saw no middle ground. Her concerns were either severe (drinking, drugs and fighting) or mild (everything else).

Donít Make a Mountain Out of a Molehill

It's also easy to fall into the trap of exaggerating your child's behavior (we'll talk more about that in Chapter Thirteen). Sometimes mild behaviors add up, and together they can seem more intolerable. It's not just that his room's a mess. It's also that he just slammed the door, used a disrespectful tone of voice and threatened to hit his sister.

Look at each behavior separately. Try not to exaggerate typical adolescent behaviors. Many mild and even moderate behaviors are a normal part of fighting for independence. Severe behaviors, especially legal and safety issues, are not. Again, lists for each individual adolescent will be different. Behaviors that are mild for Jack may be considered moderate or severe with a kid like Jill.

Finding consequences for Jill is fairly easy. Finding them for Jack is a lot tougher. You may be able to come up with only two or three that really seem to matter to him. In that case, you'll want to use them carefully. If you use those consequences for mild behaviors, they might not be as effective when it comes to severe ones. If you have one consequence that works, and you use it for everything, you'll end up not following through — you'll be too whipped. You'll be most effective with Jack if you pick one or two severe behaviors, and use that one consequence consistently with them. At least he'll know you're going to follow through with what you say.

The Whippets live in the country. One of the consequences that worked with Slug was not giving him rides to places he wanted to go. Mrs. Whippet decided that if she refused to take him anywhere because his room was a mess or because she had to constantly remind him about chores, her son would never go anywhere. Then what consequence would she use when he refused to get up for school? (Besides, he'd be home *all the time*, and that wasn't a very pleasant thought either.) So she decided to use the "no rides" consequence for school refusal, and she decided to ignore the other behaviors, temporarily.

If you target two or three of your biggest concerns, and your adolescent changes those behaviors — great. With a kid like Jack, that may be the best you can hope for. It's tempting to go back to your list and start giving out those same consequences for other, more moderate behaviors. If he changed severe behaviors, surely he'll change more moderate ones. With some adolescents, that strategy will work. In other cases, it won't. Some teens will end up sliding back into severe problems if more behaviors are targeted. Think about your child's personality. If he was using drugs and physically assaulting people, and now he's only being verbally aggressive, you may want to quit while you're ahead. You may decide to just stay consistent and continue to address only severe problems.

Mrs. Whippet ended up with several consequences that she found effective to deal with Slug's refusal to go to school. Later, she used those same consequences to start dealing with his constant habit of swearing at her. It worked. Slug actually changed not only severe behaviors, but a moderate one as well. Ms. Booker tried the same thing with Brandy. She responded to her daughter's violence with consequences that were fairly effective. Then she moved down her list to Brandy's refusal to do any chores. It backfired. Brandy fell right back into her severe behaviors. In her case, consequences worked best when they were given sparingly. Again, your adolescent's personality will determine what works best for you.

Everyone wants a piece of the pie

The moment Jack was born, he became an important part of your life — maybe the most important. When he was young, you were probably the most important influence in his life. He depended on you for almost everything: love, food, clothing, entertainment, attention and guidance. Now he's a teenager. There are all sorts of forces affecting his behavior: the media, music, peers, school, hormones. As a parent, you're probably no longer the most important influence in his life. Your piece of the pie may be just a sliver of what it used to be.

Your adolescent's peers probably influence your child's behavior more than you at this time. Peers are often less demanding, have fewer expectations and are more accepting than we are as parents. They listen, empathize and encourage each other. The media and music also take on a whole new role as Jack tries to figure out who he is, what he identifies with and believes in.

You may want to find ways to make your piece of the pie larger. Lecturing, criticizing, judging and shaming are surefire ways to make your piece smaller. Accepting your teen's personality, familiarizing yourself with things that are important to him (like music) and making positive comments to your teen will help increase your influence. Simply listening to your teen will help you get to know him, his hopes and his dreams.

After you complete the list of behaviors that concern you the most, make a list of your adolescent's strengths and positive behaviors. Believe it or not, even Jack has positive qualities and strengths. When you think of your child's strengths and positive qualities, remember them. You might even want to keep them on a note card, ready to grab, when your day seems consumed by negatives. It helps keep you balanced. And it helps your child feel better as a person. It's all in how you look at things. Some parents are able to take behaviors that once were considered negative and turn them into positive ones. Use the form in Appendix C (page 157) to help you.

A child's behavior is affected by all sorts of influences. Some of his behavior will be positive. Some of his behavior problems may be mild, moderate or severe. After you've decided into which category your child's behaviors fall, and which are truly intolerable, you'll be ready to develop some fail-proof consequences in the next chapter.

Tilt the Picture

Then take another look at it.

During one of our CRAP sessions, one parent had practiced "Changing Your Thoughts" (presented in The Thunderstorm chapter) so well that she listed one of her son's personal strengths as "his ability to argue and debate." She said he is so good at it that he would make a great defense attorney. Another parent listed one of her daughter's strengths as "being a leader," because her daughter never listens to anyone who says something she doesn't want to hear, including parents, teacher, and even her friends. This mother felt her daughter would never be a follower and she viewed this as a strong quality. And still another parent claimed her son would be a famous critic someday. "He never has anything nice to say about anyone or anything." She listed his ability to criticize *ó everything ó* as a strength.

CHAPTER ELEVEN

Consequences

*H*ere it is . . . the chapter you've been waiting for. (If you're one of the people who couldn't wait, and you're reading this chapter first, *please* go back and read the earlier chapters. This chapter will make a lot more sense when you do.)

We started talking about consequences in the last chapter. Now you've decided which behaviors you absolutely will not tolerate in your home, and you've made a list describing the severity of each behavior. You've also decided which behaviors need to be followed with a consequence. The problem is, what kind of consequence works with Jack?

Natural Consequences

The first type of consequences your adolescent will experience are *natural consequences*. Natural consequences happen as a direct result of your child's behavior and may have nothing to do with you. Slug refused to go to school, and he failed some of his classes. Brandy had sex with many different boys and caught a sexually transmitted disease. Top Dog got into fights and ended up with stitches and scars on his face. Target got caught shoplifting and was arrested.

Natural consequences are very important. They will occur

throughout your child's life, into adulthood. As a child or teenager, Jack may experience a consequence *you've* developed. He will experience natural consequences forever. It's what will help him think through his behavior. Natural consequences will influence the choices Jack makes, long after he's moved out of your home.

Parents are sometimes in the position to keep natural consequences from happening for their children. Top Dog's mom spent years "saving" her son from some natural consequences of drinking and fighting. When he was thirteen years old, a peer pressed assault charges. Top Dog's mom went to court and convinced the judge to let her son attend therapy instead of being put on probation. When Top Dog couldn't get up for school because of a hangover, his mother called to excuse him. "I had to help him," she would say. "He's my son, and he's already been through so much."

After she began attending Al-Anon meetings, Top Dog's mother realized she wasn't truly "helping" her son. She was simply rescuing him from the natural consequences that went along with his choices. Once she stopped rescuing him, Top Dog started to put more thought into his decisions. Often times he still decided to drink and fight, but at least he thought about what could happen as a result.

Responsive Consequences

The other type of consequence your adolescent will experience are *responsive consequences*. Responsive consequences are something you have control over, that you develop in *response* to a behavior or choice your child makes. Your son puts your car in the ditch while he's drunk, and you don't let him use it for a specific period of time. Your daughter calls you a bitch, and you don't give her a ride to her friend's house the next time she asks. Your son refuses to go to school, so you notify the school that you've done all you can to get him there (see Chapter Sixteen). You also stop buying him the expensive designer clothes that he wants to wear to school. Your daughter breaks her radio and television in a fit of anger, and you don't replace them (not even at Christmas). Your son puts a hole in your front door in a fit of anger, and you withhold his allowance or birthday and Christmas gifts until you've been compensated.

Responsive consequences may also be natural consequences. Your daughter steals money from your room, and you put a padlock on your door. Your daughter breaks the padlock on your door, and steals your jewelry. You report her to the police and move your valuables to a safety deposit box for the time being. Your son leaves your tools on the garage floor after he uses them without permission, and you lock them up. Your daughter punches you, and you file an assault charge.

The key to developing responsive consequences is remembering what you can control. The only thing you can control is your own response. You cannot *stop* Jack's behaviors unless he allows you to. Jill may allow you to have control by "grounding" her. In this way, you're stating, "You cannot do something," and Jill says, for the most part, "Okay, I won't." This does not include the times a teen will, of course, get away with what he or she can. Even Jill will talk on the phone before you get home when she's grounded.

Jack usually won't even give you the illusion of controlling his behavior: "Go ahead and ground me. I'm still going to that party, and *you can't stop me.*" In Jack's case, consequences you develop need to be based on your *own* behavior. . . not his. You can control only your own *response* to his behaviors.

Make a List

Think about all the things you do for your adolescent, above and beyond what you need to. You are obligated to provide food, shelter and clothing. This does not mean McDonald's, Tommy Hilfiger jeans or the latest video game. Become aware of all the "extras" you do for Jack that are a privilege, rather than a right. Those are some of the things you have control over. Make a list of them. Use Appendix D to help you (page 159).

You can't *make* Jack stay in his room if he's determined to leave the house. (Handcuffing him to the bed is considered child abuse.) On the other hand, Jack can't *make* you drive through McDonald's the next time he wants a Big Mac. The next time your adolescent refuses to do a chore, or any other "moderately" severe behavior you've identified that's intolerable but not a safety issue, control what you can. Check your list, and take away one of the "extras" you do for him every day — things that both you and your child take for granted.

If you continue to do extras for your adolescent, despite his disrespectful behavior, you are preventing him from experiencing a natural consequence. People who are disrespectful, mean or nasty to others usually don't find a lot of extra, pleasant favors from others coming their way. Jack may as well start realizing that now.

> Eight-year-old Hammer's mom brought him to therapy because he was destroying her home. He kicked holes in her doors and walls, broke windows and his possessions, and wrote all over the walls. The only consequence she had tried was "beating him," which she was "tired of." However, she continued to buy him things like a television, CD player and posters for his wall, to replace those things he destroyed during temper tantrums. Her responsive consequence of physical discipline didn't stop Hammer's behavior. When it was suggested that she use the money she would normally spend on Christmas presents to fix her home instead of buying Hammer more things to break, Hammer's expression clearly showed that it would be something that would bother him. It might make him uncomfortable enough to change his behavior. Even if he doesn't change his behavior, he is learning that consequences will follow his destructive actions.

People change their behavior because they are *uncomfortable*. If Jack is comfortable, he will probably decide he likes things the way they are. Or he simply may not care about experiencing natural consequences, and your responsive consequences may not make him uncomfortable enough to change. Jack may still feel it's "worth it" to continue his behaviors. Some pocket responses you can use for Jack that incorporate consequences are:

- "I'd like to give you a ride to your friend's house, but last time you didn't come home until two hours after curfew, so this time I won't be able to give you a ride."

- "I'd like to take you shopping with me, but I won't be able to this time because last week you got angry and broke one of the displays."

- "I'd like to drive through McDonald's right now, but you didn't do the dishes last night like I asked, so I'm using the money as a fee for my having to do the dishes. There's food in the refrigerator at home."

- "Your birthday is in two weeks, and I'd like to buy you some things. I planned on spending $_____. Unfortunately, you ran up the phone bill this month, so I'll be using $_____ of your birthday money to pay for the calls."

The most important thing about a "pocket consequence response" is following through. You can develop responses that fit your own needs: the behaviors to which you'd like to respond, and the "extras" that doing without might make your adolescent uncomfortable enough to change his behavior.

A key phrase is, ìI'd like to, but. . . î

In this way, you are simply controlling your own behavior, but in a way that may impact Jack and his comfort level.

Serious Issues and Consequences

You may be thinking to yourself, "Okay, that sounds good for *some* of the things my kid does. But what about the really big stuff? What about when he steals from me, or pushes me, or stabs his sister with a pencil? I'm supposed to respond to that by not taking him to McDonald's? I don't think so."

You're right. Safety and legal issues need more serious responsive consequences. Here are examples of such issues:

- Your adolescent continues to destroy your property or home.

- Your adolescent harms you or another family member physically, in a way that is assaultive (punching, using any type of weapon, choking, or anything else that could result in serious harm).

- Your adolescent steals from you on more than one occasion.

- Your adolescent refuses to go to school.

- Your adolescent breaks the law in any other way, such as using drugs, running away, or staying out past city curfew.

In these cases, Jack's behaviors would be considered severe. You will probably need to involve community agencies such as the court, police, school, and/or mental health and substance abuse facilities. If your child breaks the law, it is very appropriate to involve your local police. If he assaults you, file charges. If he assaults his siblings, ask the police to come to your home and talk with your child. File charges if that doesn't work.

Involving the police and court as part of your responsive consequences could mean your adolescent ends up on probation. You might consider this to be a natural consequence of his illegal behavior, however, it may lead you to feel guilty or sorry for your teen. So be prepared. Remember, saving him from natural consequences could be more harmful in the long run. In the adult world, it might not be probation, it might be prison.

If your child refuses to go to school, involve the school staff. Take steps to protect yourself, so that your child is the one who experiences natural consequences for his decision – not you. These will usually be in the form of failing, truancy charges or probation. Chapter Seventeen will show you how to use these community agencies to protect yourself, and, at the same time, provide Jack with natural and responsive consequences that are appropriate to severe behaviors.

How to Choose a Consequence

Things to consider when choosing a responsive consequence:

1. *Are you responding to your adolescent while you're emotional?* If you're feeling angry, hurt or frustrated, wait until later to choose the consequence. You can let your adolescent know by saying, "I'm upset right now and need time to determine how I'm going to respond to your behavior. I'll let you know when I've decided what I'm going to do."

2. *Is the consequence fair?* Does it fit the severity of the behavior? You may want to come back to this question after reading Chapter Thirteen on exaggerating and minimizing.

3. *Has your adolescent already received a consequence?* It may be unnecessary for him to be given a second consequence. For example, if your child swore at the teacher, he probably already experienced a natural consequence, like school detention. Is it necessary to provide a responsive consequence yourself?

4. *Have you developed a fail-proof consequence?* When developing a fail-proof consequence, it may be helpful to think about what your teen likes, or things he wants and asks for. Fail-proof consequences are very difficult to come up with when you deal with someone like Jack. You might be able to find only one or two effective consequences. If that's all you have, use it *carefully* and *consistently.*

How to Develop a Fail-proof Consequence

1. *Start by selecting a consequence you think may be fail-proof.* Be specific. What is the exact length of time the consequence will be given for? When will it start and end?

2. *Now, check it, to see if it is fail-proof.* List the *possible reactions*

your adolescent may have to this consequence. List all you can think of, covering as many scenarios as possible. If you choose to respond to his behavior of breaking curfew by not giving him rides anywhere for the week, what might he do in response? Hitchhike? Steal your car and drive himself? Steal someone else's car? Walk?

3. *Do you still have control over the consequence?* After each of your adolescent's possible reactions ask yourself if you still have control over this consequence. Remember, you can control only your own behavior, so if the consequence depends on your adolescent going along with it, it isn't fail-proof. (Example: If you use grounding as a consequence and one of your child's possible reactions is to climb out the window and leave anyway, who has control over this consequence? Your child.)

4. *Is this a consequence you can live with?*

   • After listing each of your child's reactions (the ones that you've decided still leave you in control), ask yourself if this is a reaction you can live with. If not, you may end up suffering more than your child, and your consequence will probably fail.

   Adolescents are very good at knowing how to make a parent suffer after giving a consequence. Slug once said, ìIf my mom says I canít go somewhere, I just turn up the bass on my stereo really loud. I get it so loud her things fall off the shelves and break. She ends up telling me to get out of the house.î If you have to go back on a consequence after itís been given, it will reinforce to your teen that he has control over the situation.

   • Remember, your child will *choose* how to respond to your consequence. If you refuse to take him anywhere for a week, and he steals your car, a natural consequence of that illegal behavior is that you will call the police. Bottom line — you remained in control of the consequence by not taking him anywhere for a week.

The key to coming up with a fail-proof consequence is to determine whether or not you have total control over it. That means it must be based on your behavior — not your adolescent's. We have provided an example of developing fail-proof consequences in Appendix D (page 159).

Get Ready

Hopefully, you will be able to come up with at least one fail-proof consequence. Before you start using it, a couple of things need to be considered.

- It's going to take a lot of work and commitment (and possibly nerves of steel) on your part to follow through with the consequence you are giving.

- If your child is like Jack, he will do everything in his power to get you to give up on this consequence. DON'T GIVE UP! The key to whether or not this consequence is successful depends on your follow-through.

You may want to begin by choosing only *one* behavior, the most severe one on your behavior list, and use *one* fail-proof consequence. Focus totally on your follow-through and be consistent. Being consistent means that if your child repeats the same behavior, use that same consequence again. (A=B. If your child does A, he can count on you to respond with B.)

CHAPTER TWELVE

Tug of War Will Give You Rope Burn

There's nothing Jack loves more than a good power struggle. It's challenging. It's exciting. It's fun. Most of all, it's something he's good at. The subject isn't important. It's the debate he loves. He'll engage in a tug of war with anyone . . . a teacher, principal, therapist, or someone on the street. But you're his favorite player. Why? Maybe because he knows how to get you to tug on that rope. Maybe because he likes to see your emotional reaction. Maybe because you're pretty good at power struggles, and you make a good opponent. Maybe you're just around more than anyone else. Who knows? We see the lightning, but we have no idea what's in the clouds.

The Power Dance

Adolescents are notorious for engaging parents in a *power dance*. You may be minding your own business, enjoying a rare peaceful moment, and your son walks in. He's bored, spiteful, or in the mood to feel powerful. He plops down next to you and says casually, "I'm going to get my tongue pierced next week." (Translation: Would you like to dance?)

You look up, dismayed and fearful, thinking of how you'll explain this to friends and family. You reply, "Oh, no, you're not." (Translation: Sure, I'll dance with you).

Your son cocks his head, physically puffs up, and says confidently, "Oh, yes, I am. I already saved the money." (Translation: Isn't this fun? I'm not bored anymore.)

The dance is in full swing now, as your son leads you across the floor, stepping on your toes all the way. Your face gets hot, and adrenalin pumps as you reply angrily, "Well, you're under eighteen, and I am NOT signing the permission slip. Besides, don't you know how dangerous that can be? Do you want to look like a freak?"

The two of you continue in the power dance until someone either gets tired and gives up, gets angry and stomps off, or the situation escalates. More explosive subjects get brought up, things snowball and may even get violent.

A power struggle begins with a battle for control. It comes from the need to have the upper hand, the final say or to be the one who is right. A difference in opinion can come down to, "I'm right and you're wrong. There's only one way to do things in this situation, and *it's my way*." Power struggles can be very destructive. If Jack is spending all of his time trying to gain control, he won't learn how to think his actions through. He'll be too busy trying to win a tug of war. A parent can waste valuable time and emotional energy trying to hang on to that upper hand.

Control

Many books, even therapists, take the approach of trying to help a parent regain power and control. We went browsing one day in a popular bookstore. On a shelf in the parenting section, we found a book with a title similar to *Taking Back Your Control*. It was all about how parents need to regain authority over their adolescents. It was full of suggestions on how to control your teenager. You know the ones: take away his radio, ground him, don't let him talk on the phone. If he threatens to run away, take away his clothes so he can't leave the house. On the very next shelf in the self-help section (we swear this is true) there was a book for adults who have trouble making their own decisions? Why do these adults doubt themselves? According to that book, *their parents were too controlling.*

Power struggles can easily escalate to the point of physical aggression as a way to show who, in fact, is more powerful. Ms. Booker and Mrs. Whippet both found themselves in power struggles with their teenagers. In both cases, physical violence was the result. Ms. Booker tried to control Brandy's behaviors of staying out past curfew and ignoring house rules. Brandy responded with physical aggression, pushing or hitting her mother. In a power struggle, she physically overpowered her mother. On the other hand, Slug simply refused to get out of bed; he ignored Mrs. Whippet. He proved he had the ultimate control over whether or not he went to school. Mrs. Whippet tried to gain control over Slug's behavior — control he wouldn't give her. She became so frustrated that she pulled his hair, kicked and slapped him. Even then, physical force didn't work.

When your teen tries to engage you in a power struggle, or *asks you to dance,* you have a choice. You can dance or you can sit that one out. If you choose to dance, be prepared to come away feeling tired, frustrated, angry and hurt. That's the nature of a power struggle. Even if you think you've won. Think hard before you dance. It may be one of your teen's favorite recreational activities, and he's probably very good at it. Just call him Fred Astaire.

Donít Pick Up the Rope

Think back to the thunderstorm chapter. *If you canít change the situation, change the way you think about it.* This is a chance to use that technique. If you *think* your child is trying to make you angry or just wants to argue, you'll probably *feel* angry, irritated or resentful. It may push one of your emotional buttons. You'll *act* by engaging in a power struggle. But, if you can *think* differently, you'll *feel* differently. "My child is asking me to dance. He may be bored or in a bad mood. His behavior may not even have anything to do with me." You'll *feel* calm. You won't dance.

Remember, you probably don't have the full story. You don't know what kind of day your adolescent has experienced while out in his world. You may not have a clue about his thoughts or feelings at that moment. You recognize the lightning, but you don't necessarily know what's in the dark clouds. All you see is his action: trying to pick a fight or irritate you, *asking you to dance.*

This is also a good chance to *model* for your teen how to handle others calmly and rationally, rather than engaging in a fight. He may not choose to follow your example, but you will have done what you can as a parent. It also saves you from being called a hypocrite later: "Why shouldn't I yell if I'm mad? You do." Kids have good memories. So take a minute to mentally relax a little. Try not to jump to conclusions, so you can get a better idea of what's really going on with your child. Adolescents often overreact or exaggerate. Sometimes they get caught up in emotion, just like adults.

As a parent, you may be in a good position to de-escalate, or calm, Jack's behavior. After all, you know him best. You've lived with him, and watched his personality develop. You've seen him at his worst and his best. You know what *his* emotional buttons are, guaranteed to escalate, or worsen, his mood and behavior. You probably installed some of them. Which are they? For some, blaming, challenging, threatening, criticizing, ignoring or "rubbing it in," may be surefire ways to get an angry teen angrier. The same problem may be de-escalated by validating his feelings. This means simply listening, letting him rant and rave, and acknowledging what you think he is feeling: "You seem really upset."

What escalates Jack may de-escalate Jill. Ignoring a teen who is yelling or trying to pick a control battle may calm one, but make another angrier. You can strengthen your awareness of how to avoid escalating your emotional child. Sit down and make a list of responses that seem to make things better or worse. Does your adolescent respond better if you ignore his mood or provide the opportunity to talk? Keep your child's personal strengths in mind when doing this. For instance, if one of your daughter's strengths is her sense of humor, you may be able to use appropriate, non-shaming humor to de-escalate a situation. *No teasing.*

You may want to have some handy pocket responses ready the next time you seem to be getting drawn into a power struggle or control battle:

- "I understand how you're thinking about this issue. You know, there can be more than one way to look at things."

- "You certainly have a right to your opinion, and I respect that."

- "You know what? I appreciate your position, but I'm not in the mood to debate this at this time."

- "I hear what you're saying."

Getting Your Adolescent to Think

Of all the things you can do for your child, showing him how to think a behavior through, before acting, is the most important. He may not always make choices you agree with, but at least you'll know he is making conscious decisions. Power struggles keep a teen reacting to you, rather than strengthening his problem-solving skills. If Jack is busy trying to win a tug-of-war, he won't think his behaviors through to possible consequences. And that's not good.

Once Mrs. Whippet found her middle ground, she stopped buying into Slug's attempts to engage in power struggles.

One day Slug strolled into the kitchen and announced, "I decided what I'm going to do to make money. I'm gonna sell drugs."

She was prepared. She simply looked at him calmly, and said, "Let me know how that works for you."

Slug, confused, walked away. He didn't get the reaction he anticipated. The power dance never even began.

Ms. Booker also handled power struggles differently, once she found middle ground.

When Brandy came home and yelled, "I'm gonna kick the shit out of that girl at school," her mom was ready for her.

She began by recognizing and validating Brandy's feelings by saying, "Boy, you sound really mad."

Brandy fumed, "I am. She's pissing me off. Tomorrow she's gonna be laying on the floor needing an ambulance."

Ms. Booker replied, "And then what?"

When Brandy had trouble coming up with what might happen next as a result of her behavior, her mother simply asked questions.

"Could you get suspended?"

"Yeah, probably."

"Could the police be called?"

"I doubt it."

When Brandy disagreed, her mom didn't argue or try to prove her point. She simply said, "I just wondered."

Brandy continued to think the situation through, and ended with the possibility she might go to jail for assault. Then she grabbed the phone and called her friend to talk about it some more. There was no power dance, because it wasn't a struggle for control. Ms. Booker saw her daughter's lightning, but didn't make assumptions about what was in the clouds. In doing so, she helped her daughter to think through her behavior without getting drawn into an argument or power struggle. If Ms. Booker had responded to Brandy by saying something like, "Don't you use that kind of language in front of me" or "Oh no, you won't," the dance would have begun. Brandy may not have thought things through for herself.

The Defensive Disco

Sometimes the hardest power struggles to avoid are the defensive discos; the times when Jack criticizes *you*. The topic is always personal. It may be your looks, parenting skills, intelligence, or any number of things. His biggest dilemma is which button to push. The goal is always the same: to put you on the defensive. The defensive disco typically goes something like this:

You've recently given your adolescent a consequence for something he's done. Or maybe you're just sitting there, minding your own business. He walks in, wearing his *Saturday*

Night Fever white disco suit. You can almost hear the seventies' music in the background. He says something like, "I wish Dad was still here. He would've stuck around, if you hadn't been such a bitch to him."

For a minute, you're blinded by the strobe lights. You say defensively, "You know that's not why your dad left. He's an alcoholic. I tried to make it work, but he didn't want to. Besides, he could call or come see you any time he wants." Your child pushed your guilt button. The dance has begun.

It can be an automatic reaction to defend yourself when you're personally attacked. You want the other person to know, "Hey, it's not like that." The problem is, Jack doesn't care. He's not at all interested in your answer. If he were, he'd say something like, "I miss dad. Why isn't he around anymore?"

You don't have to defend yourself. You can talk until you're blue in the face, and Jack still won't hear you. If you find you are defending yourself, it's a safe bet you're out on the dance floor, moving to the beat of a Bee Gees tune. The defensive disco is the same as any other power dance. It's just cleverly disguised. (Oh, by the way . . . the dance isn't quite over yet. Put on your comfortable shoes and get ready for the real "zingers" coming up in the next chapter!)

CHAPTER THIRTEEN

Zingers

Years of living with Jack can make a parent nervous. You start to walk around on eggshells, wondering what's in store for you next. "What's he going to set me up for this time? Which trap am I going to fall into next?" You can probably picture yourself walking in the jungle. Jack's in the tree above, wearing a safari hat, waiting to drop a net on you.

Believe it or not, the "parent traps" we tend to fall into the most are the ones we set for ourselves. We call these parent traps *zingers*, and they're what keep you dancing with Jack. Let's get to know them better.

Personalizing

Personalizing is the biggest parent trap out there. It means taking your adolescent's words or behavior *personally*. Jack comes home from school and throws his book bag in the middle of the living room floor.

You ask him to take care of it – pick it up and put it in his room.

He yells back at you, "In a minute, all right."

Taking this personally, you respond angrily, "Hey. Don't yell at me like that. I don't deserve that kind of disrespect."

When you personalize things, you assume you have something to do with another person's behavior. The problem is that's usually not the case. Remember the thunderstorm? When you see the lightning, you don't know what's in the clouds. Personalizing happens when you assume that whatever's in the clouds has something to do with you. When Jack talks to you in a nasty, hateful way, it may not have anything to do with how he feels toward you. He may be angry about something that happened at school, with his friends or a number of other things that happened in his day. The lightning may not have anything to do with you. You're just in its path.

Adolescence is a very self-centered time. And let's not forget those notorious teenage hormones. If something was upsetting at school, your child probably brings that emotion home with him. If he's tired, he's probably irritable. Adolescents typically don't have the maturity to change their moods, just because they've left a situation. Neither do many adults, for that matter. When you have a bad day at work, how easy is it to *leave it at the office*? It's not any easier for teenagers.

Target is a fourteen-year-old young man. He's on probation and in foster care for shoplifting and truancy. To be released to his parents, he must attend school and follow certain rules. When Target started skipping school to see his new girlfriend, his parents took it very personally. Because his parents personalized Target's behavior, they became angry, hurt and disappointed. "Why are you doing this? Don't you want to come home to us? You must not, or you wouldn't keep doing these things."

Actually, Target wanted to go home very much. He also wanted to see his girlfriend very much. He decided to skip school based on what he wanted *at that moment*, which was to see his girlfriend. His behavior was self-centered. Hormones had something to do with it, too. His decision had nothing to do with his parents. They assumed it did. They *personalized* his behavior.

Ms. Booker suffers from terrible migraine headaches.

Some days she can't even get up off the couch. On one of these days, Brandy made it clear she was going to a party. Her mom said to her nicely, "I need you to stay here and help me. I'm sick." Brandy stormed off to her room, screaming, "I can't believe you're trying to make me stay here. I hate you."

Ms. Booker took Brandy's words very personally. "You don't even care that I'm so sick. I can't believe you're my daughter. What a selfish brat you are."

Brandy's words and behavior were completely self-centered. She was thinking of only herself, and how her plans for the night might be ruined. It wasn't necessarily that she didn't care about her mother. She just cared about herself more. That's very typical of children and adolescents. When Ms. Booker personalized her daughter's tantrum, she felt hurt, angry and disappointed. She ended up feeling bad physically *and* emotionally.

The Thunderstorm technique can help you avoid the *personalizing parent trap*. Changing your thoughts will change your feelings, so you can respond differently. If you *think* Jack's behavior is personal, toward you, you'll *feel* angry, upset and hurt. If you can *think* his behavior has nothing to do with you personally, you'll *feel* better. You'll act calmer, too. Some examples of things you can tell yourself are:

- "This isn't personal."

- "He's thinking of only himself."

- "This isn't necessarily about me."

- "My child is feeling really hateful but I'm not going to respond."

You may even be able to feel sorry for your child, who is obviously having a hateful day. (Being hateful doesn't feel good.) At the very least, you'll stop experiencing all those unpleasant emotions you have when you take Jack's behavior personally.

There are times when your child's behavior may truly be directed at you. What's in the clouds (above the lightning) may actually have something to do with how he's thinking or feeling about you. If it sounds like a personal attack, it might be. When Top Dog growled at his mother, "God you get on my nerves. Why don't you get a life?" he meant it. She did get on his nerves. He did want her to get her own life, so she'd stop trying to control his drinking.

Keep in mind the emotional buttons your adolescent may target. Which ones really *get* to you? Anger? Fear? Guilt? Slug once told Mrs. Whippet she was "the worst mother in the world." Obviously, he was exaggerating. But it worked; he pushed one of her buttons. She went right into the defensive disco. Why? Mrs. Whippet was still carrying a load of guilt around because Slug doesn't know his "real" dad. She wasn't even aware she had that guilt. All she knew was that when Slug told her she was "the worst mother," it *got* to her. She took it personally.

When your child is in a mean, nasty, "I'm fourteen and the world sucks" kind of mood, there's a good chance he'll take it out on you. He'll make a crack about you personally. He'll call you a name. He'll get mouthy. If his behavior really *gets* to you, figure out why. Otherwise you'll take it personally, and react in anger. You'll be out on the dance floor before you know it.

Some teens speak and act impulsively, without thinking of how their words will affect you. An honest reflection of your own feelings may work with Jill: "It makes me angry and hurts my feelings when you call me names." This will *not* work if your child is personally attacking you in an attempt to get the focus off of his own behavior. It will *not* work if his motivation is to push your emotional buttons. Reflecting your feelings in those cases will only make the situation worse and prove his strategy worked. You'll reflect your feelings honestly, he'll make another mean comment, and you'll get mad.

A pocket response to personal attacks may be "I'm sorry you feel the need to call me names," or "I'm sorry you feel the need to criticize me." This does several things. It avoids making the situation worse. It models a calm response to a confrontation. It keeps him from knowing he's pushed an emotional button. Most important, you won't be personalizing his behavior, so you won't have all those unpleasant emotions.

Exaggerating

Everyone exaggerates from time to time. Jack certainly does. As parents, so do we. Adolescents are quick to point out when parents overreact: "You didn't have to get so mad, what I did wasn't that bad," or "God, mom, you get mad about every little thing." Sure you do. You're tired. You're frustrated. You're ready for what's going to come *next* from your kid.

Target's mom was exhausted. Her son wanted to get off probation, but kept making poor choices (including skipping school to see his girlfriend). He didn't always turn in his homework, so he was getting Ds and Es in school. On the other hand, he no longer shoplifted, and he hadn't been in a fight in over a month. After almost a year in foster care, he earned the privilege of a week-long home visit.

Mom came to a therapy session, upset and frustrated. The biggest problem of the week, one that she just couldn't get past was: *crotch rot.* "He's been home for almost a week, and he hasn't given me any dirty underwear to wash. I know he hasn't changed it once all week. He'll probably get crotch rot." She was ready to send him back to the foster home early.

While the thought of a teenager wearing the same underwear for four days is certainly . . . stinky . . . there are ways to put it in perspective. There's no documentation of anyone dying from crotch rot. Insurance companies don't write policies that accept or deny crotch rot claims. Doctors don't open practices specializing in crotch rot. The worst scenario is probably that Target might start to smell. People won't want to be around him, which might make him uncomfortable enough to change his underwear. Because she was exhausted and emotional, mom was a little too sensitive to her son's behavior. She fell into the parent trap of exaggerating. The result: she was ready to cut short a home visit, something Target had earned by making positive changes.

Eight-year-old Hammer's mom decided he needed to be taken out of her home, because he was dangerous. Why? "He told me he has nightmares sometimes about killing people. What if he actually does it some day?"

Hammer's mom was overwhelmed. She felt her son needed to be

in "boot camp." She started exaggerating Hammer's behavior, looking for a reason to justify sending him there. She exaggerated to the point that her son couldn't even share his dreams with her.

There's never been a perfect parent, at least not one we've ever heard of. There are bound to be times when you exaggerate your child's behavior . . . and your own. Top Dog's mom found that her favorite trap was exaggerating her own faults as a parent, and said, "I shouldn't have yelled at him and called him a loser that time when he came home late. I'm a horrible parent. No wonder my son is so screwed up." Once she found middle ground, she was able to be more realistic about herself, and said, "I wish I hadn't yelled at him, but I'm not perfect. I'm doing the best I can. Next time I'll respond to Top Dog more calmly."

Today, society in general is in a state of overreaction. Just ask any kid how to get a few days off school, and they'll reply, "Say you're going to kill someone." Finding middle ground is the key. Which brings us to our next parent trap . . .

Minimizing

Trying to avoid the exaggerating parent trap is good. Just be careful not to fall into the opposite trap: *minimizing*. Minimizing means seeing a behavior as less serious than it truly is.

Jill is a "good kid." Ask her to do something, and she will – with a smile. She does things with her mom, "respects" her parents, gets good grades and has never been in trouble at school. Teachers love her. Her brother Jack gets on her nerves, but he gets on everyone's nerves. Sometimes she yells back at him, but mostly she just goes in her room.

One night Jill hit a tree while driving her dad's car. She was drunk. Luckily, she had only a few cuts and bruises. Because they'd never had any "real" problems with Jill, her parents minimized the incident. "Well, she was out with friends. You know how kids are. They had a few drinks. We're just going to let this one slide." They minimized a behavior that was a safety issue – not to mention a legal problem.

Minimizing isn't just a danger with Jill. You can fall into the same trap with any child. Strangely enough, we often tend to exaggerate minor behaviors, while minimizing the more serious problems. Finding that middle ground is the best you can hope for.

Rationalizing

Rationalizing is the twin brother to minimizing. It means trying to explain someone else's behavior. You try to give a logical answer to the question "Why did he do that?" People rationalize their own behavior every day. Jack's a professional at rationalizing: there's a reason behind everything he does. Just ask.

Adolescents are good enough at justifying their behavior, and they don't need parents helping them out. Sixteen-year-old Firebug was a young man with a history of severe behavioral problems. The list included shooting another kid with an air rifle, threatening to kill classmates and getting into fights every week. He often made sexual comments that made girls nervous. He'd been expelled from school because of his behavior.

When Firebug came to therapy, he'd just been released from a residential treatment center, where he'd been for three years. He'd been on probation just as long and was still on it. Mom explained that Firebug really didn't need therapy, but a judge had ordered him to come. She told the story of how her son had been "railroaded."

It seems that when Firebug was thirteen years old, he and a neighbor boy were hanging out in the backyard. The neighbor was "kind of a friend, but not really." There was a history of conflict between the two boys. There was a barrel in the yard, and they decided to light a fire in it. Firebug threw some lighter fluid on the neighbor's pants, and they caught on fire. The boy was hospitalized. He said Firebug had thrown the fluid on him in a moment of anger. Firebug was charged with reckless endangerment and sentenced to three years of probation and residential treatment.

Firebug said very little in the therapy session. Mom did the talking for him. She told of how the fire was "really just an accident. You see, the boys had seen an older neighbor lighting a fire in *his* barrel, so *of course* they decided to try the same thing." She continued, "The other boy and the neighbors all lied on my son, so he would get in trouble." Mom even took it a step further and rationalized her son's behavior to the point of making him into a hero: "Actually Firebug saved the other kid's life. He threw water on him and put the fire out."

She also had an answer for Firebug's history of fighting and school problems: "Well, he really doesn't *want* to hit the other kids. But they say bad things about me to him, and it gets him mad. He ends up fighting because he can't help it." Besides, "The school lies, too. They just want to get rid of him."

Mom obviously had a tough time accepting the seriousness of her son's actions. She fell into two parent traps at once: minimizing and rationalizing. She tried to convince herself, and others, that Firebug's behavior wasn't really dangerous. She explained *why* he was aggressive, too. Firebug's expression in therapy showed that he knew exactly how serious his problems were. During his mom's speech, he rolled his eyes and shook his head. She couldn't even convince *him* that his behavior was okay.

Mom missed a good opportunity to use the modeling technique with her son. She could have responded to his behavior without minimizing, rationalizing or exaggerating. She could have responded to his early behaviors by saying, "I know it upsets you when people say things about me, but violence is not the answer. You could seriously hurt someone, or be badly hurt yourself. It's also assault, which is against the law. What other ways could you handle your feelings that are less dangerous?"

There are times when parents minimize and rationalize their *own* behavior: "I didn't mean to hit my son, but I was so angry. He pushed it past the limit and was asking for it. It's not that bad of a bruise. I'm sorry about it, but he never should have said those things to me."

Instead of minimizing and rationalizing, you can model a way of looking at your own behavior that shows a middle ground: "I made a mistake when I bruised my son. I was angry about his behavior, but that doesn't justify the way I hurt him physically. Next time, I'll be more aware of my anger, so I can leave the situation before I reach that point again." It will provide the opportunity for your adolescent to learn from your responses. You're modeling how to look at a situation realistically, without falling into any traps. That's a valuable skill.

CHAPTER FOURTEEN

Did I Say That Out Loud?

Eight-year-old Hammer's mom took him to therapy. Her biggest concern was Hammer's behavior whenever he got angry. "He hits, he steals and he lies. He goes into rages. He has kicked holes in my walls. I'm ready to put him in foster care." Mom wanted Hammer to learn how to handle anger without physical violence.

"I tell him all the time to just walk away," she sighed. "I work forty hours a week. I just don't have the time to be out in the middle of the street all night, fighting with these neighbor kids' mamas." When asked what consequences she'd tried with her son, Mom replied, "I tried beating him, but he just doesn't seem to care."

Did she hear what she just said? Did she just model a violent approach to anger and frustration? You bet. Does she understand that? Probably not. Unless you're really paying attention, it's hard to hear yourself. Especially when you're in the middle of an emotional situation.

Letís Get Ready to Rumble!

Fifteen-year-old Slammer's mom had trouble hearing herself, too. "He just gets so violent," she said in a therapy session. "We watch that 'WWE Wrestling' all the time. It's one of the things the kids all like to do. Anyway, we know all the moves now, and we get each other in different holds when we play around. But Slammer, he gets rough. He'll get one of us in a neck hold, and it *hurts*."

Slammer said, "Well, you guys hurt me. I don't get mad like that until somebody gets me in some hold where my legs are stretched up over my head. And you guys won't let go."

Mom replied, "Oh, come on, Slammer. You know we do the same thing to your brother, and he doesn't whine and cry like you do. We're just having fun. You take it too far."

"Well," he says one last time. "That's what makes me mad, and that's when I get rough."

Mom couldn't hear what Slammer was trying to tell her. Even more so, she couldn't hear how she contradicted herself.

Listen to Yourself

Remember how we talked about modeling in Chapter Six? It's the most powerful tool in your parenting kit. Modeling is the chance to show your child how to behave, by the things you say and do. Listening to yourself is the key. If you tell your child not to lie, don't call in sick to work when you're really not. If you tell your child not to disrespect you by yelling, don't shout at him when you lose your temper. If you do, two things happen. One, it contradicts what you just told him. Two, it gives him a chance to push the *blame* emotional button. "I'm yelling because you're yelling." Jack will push your buttons enough without you handing him an extra opportunity.

One of the biggest concerns parents come to therapy with is a child's physical aggression. Slammer and Hammer are true examples of children who handle anger violently. In both cases, their parents modeled that violence. If you expect your adolescent to express his anger without violence, you must model this expectation for him. If Hammer is to understand that his behavior is *assaultive*, and can result in police involvement, it must be clear that *anyone* who is violent (including a parent), is being assaultive. If you expect Jack to handle things nonviolently, that expectation must extend to all family members. The *house rules* will include *no violence*. Jack still controls whether or not he will meet this expectation. More importantly, as a parent, your responsibility is to model it.

We all have times that we completely contradict ourselves. The point is not to beat yourself up about it but to recognize when it happens. It may even be a chance for humor. Being more aware of the messages you're sending to your teenager, by both words and actions, will give you more control. You'll be able to take advantage of chances to model the behavior you hope to see from your child. You'll stay on your TOES.

Now that we've encouraged you to take responsibility for your own words and actions, let's take a look at how teenagers often avoid responsibility themselves.

CHAPTER FIFTEEN

The Blame Game

Not only is Jack a professional at getting you to dance, he's an expert at playing games. His favorite is *The Blame Game*. If you're the parent of an adolescent, you've probably heard the phrases, "I didn't do it" and "It's not my fault." You may even hear them in your sleep.

It Wasnít Me!

Parents often worry when an adolescent has trouble accepting responsibility. Ms. Booker said to Brandy's therapist, "She needs to start taking responsibility for her own behavior. She blames everyone else for her problems."

Of course she does. It's human nature. How many five year olds do you know who would say, "Yes, mommy, I ate the cookies after you told me not to"? How many fifteen year olds do you know who would come home and say, "Dad, I got drunk at a party last night. I know I need to take responsibility for my actions"? How many adults do you know who simply accept responsibility for their own mistakes, without *any* rationalizing or blaming? People have difficulty doing so, no matter what their age.

When your adolescent tries to blame you for one of his choices (such as refusing to go to school), he's asking you to play a game, like

Monopoly. He picks up the dice and rolls: "I missed school today because you didn't wake me up." He moves his token and passes the dice to you.

You pick up the dice and roll: "I did too wake you up. You wouldn't get out of bed." You move your token, land on his property and have to pay him rent. You pass the dice back to him.

He rolls: "Uh-uh. I fell back asleep and you never came back in." He passes the dice.

You roll: "I did too. I tried to get you up three times today. It's not my fault you missed school." He smiles. Why? Because he owns Boardwalk and Park Place, and you keep landing on his hotels.

When your adolescent tries to get you to play The Blame Game, you can respond in several ways. You can play and lose. You can refuse to pick up the dice by ignoring the invitation to play. Or you can use a pocket response, such as, "I'm sorry you had a hard time making it to school today. Do you have any ideas on how tomorrow could be different?"

Thirteen-year-old Spice loved to play The Blame Game. According to her, someone else was always responsible for her behavior: skipping school, running away from home and refusing to follow anyone's rules. Her mother and stepfather had been married two years. In a therapy session, her stepfather said angrily, "We haven't even been able to take a honeymoon yet because of her behavior. If my wife would be stricter with Spice, we wouldn't be having all these problems."

Without even realizing it, he modeled for his stepdaughter exactly how to blame others.

The ìRî Word ó Taking Responsibility

As parents, we can be just as good at playing The Blame Game as Jack. Fourteen-year-old Target's father went to a therapy session and said, "I just don't know what to do about Target. I'm an alcoholic, and I've been sober for ten years. But my nerves are so shot that I'm ready to drink again. I think he needs to know what he's driving me to do." He rationalized any future drinking relapse he might have by blaming his son.

Remember, your child is not responsible for your emotional well-being. If you're having trouble coping with stress related to your child, you have an opportunity to model. You can take responsibility for your own behavior by not blaming him for your emotional state. Go to therapy, join a support group or do whatever it takes to strengthen your coping skills. It will show your child that you are taking responsibility for yourself.

Our children are the ones for whom we have the most expectations. When those expectations aren't met, it's natural to look for a source of blame. Who or what can be held responsible for our disappointment? We may blame ourselves and feel guilty: "I can't believe my son swore at me like that. Where did I go wrong?" Or we may decide our child is to blame and wonder what's wrong with him: "I can't believe he swore at me. He has no respect for me or anyone else." We may even blame the environment: "That's it. He never swore at me until he started hanging around that one friend of his."

Holding your adolescent responsible for his actions is a good thing. Blaming him is not. Unfortunately, The Blame Game has no winners.

Shame

Just a few steps away from blame is another, more dangerous parent trap: shame. Fourteen-year-old Target's parents were angry, frustrated, disappointed and sometimes disgusted by his behavior. He knew it. Whenever Target and his father were in a room together, Dad's voice took on a shaming tone similar to that of a great-great-grandmother from The Old Country. The only thing missing was the phrase, "You should be ashamed of yourself." It wasn't needed – the tone said it all.

Target's dad responded to his son's negative behavior out of emotion. He responded while he was feeling angry, frustrated and disappointed. His response made it clear he wanted his son to feel guilty and ashamed of himself. The problem was that Target already felt badly about himself. He continued to make poor choices, feeling more and more ashamed. Soon a cycle started. Target would make a poor choice, Dad would shame him, and Target would respond by acting up even more.

Ms. Booker tried to shame Brandy about her negative behaviors. Brandy used her mother's tone and words to rationalize her choices: "Oh, well, I'm just a screw up, right? So what's it matter what I do? If you're *so* disappointed in me, maybe I should just leave."

In both cases, Target and Brandy didn't respond the way their parents had expected. Neither will Jack. You will not change your adolescent's behavior by trying to shame him. It will backfire and leave *you* feeling whipped when you go to bed at night.

Tabulations: ìWaitress, may I have my tab?î

A tabulation is the mental list of your child's past wrong doings that you keep in your back pocket, at the ready. You may pull up this list at any time. You may not even be aware you're doing it.

There were times when Ms. Booker actually hated her daughter. Part of the reason she felt so strongly had to do with the running tab she kept of Brandy's mistakes. It went something like this:

- "I couldn't go anywhere when Brandy was little, because she would throw screaming temper tantrums wherever we went. She embarrassed me all the time."

- "When Brandy was ten, she stole money out of my purse."

- "She caught the house on fire one day because she was smoking and didn't put the cigarette out all the way."

- "The police have come to my house at least five times because Brandy stays out past curfew, or gets into trouble with her friends."

- "When she was twelve, I went out on the first date I'd had in months. She had her friends over, got drunk, and trashed my house. I haven't been out again since."

- "Last week, Brandy called me a bitch and told me to stay out of her life. She's always saying things she knows will hurt me. She doesn't care about my feelings."

Each time Brandy made a poor choice or intentionally hurt Ms. Booker, "The List" popped into her mother's mind. Ms. Booker believed her daughter had no remorse for any of the things she said or did. (In reality, sometimes Brandy was sorry and sometimes she wasn't.) Because Ms. Booker wasn't able to let go of the past, she kept waiting for an apology from Brandy that never came.

You may not think you have a mental list of things you believe your child has done wrong over the years, but take a minute to really think about it. Do any of Jack's escapades continue to pop into your mind, leaving you angry, hurt or resentful? Do you ever think he owes you an apology for all the ways you believe he's mistreated you? If so, you're still carrying the past around with you. No wonder you're whipped. Tabulations are a heavy load, and will leave you exhausted. In order to lighten that load you may need to forgive some things that you once felt were unforgivable. Stop waiting for Jack to apologize. It's not going to happen. Keeping a tab is like a credit card. You're the one who ends up paying — with lots of interest tacked on.

Kids can be professionals at keeping tabs on parents. Thirteen-year-old Spice had a running tabulation of every mistake her mother had ever made. Whenever the focus was on her own behavior, Spice would pull out her version of The List:

- "Remember the time you drove drunk with me in the car? You almost killed us."

- "Remember the time you wouldn't let me talk to my friend on the phone, and she died in a car accident the next day? I'll never forgive you for that."

- "Remember the time you called me a bitch?"

- "Remember the time you brought that man home from the bar and slept with him?"

Mom's reaction was usually to go right into the Defensive Disco: "I said I was sorry about that, Spice. I haven't done anything like that in a long time." When an adolescent starts listing all the wrongs he feels you've committed, he's likely to push your emotional buttons, particularly the guilt button. Spice and her mother spent hours dancing like this, and it kept the focus off Spice's behavior.

Unconditional Love

It's easy to get caught up in blame and tabulation, whether you're a teenager or an adult. Both occur in many types of relationships: parent and child, marriages, friendships. In some cases, it can seem impossible to overcome past hurts. If you want your relationship with Jack to be healthier, getting over those past hurts is essential.

You've probably experienced every feeling imaginable with Jack. There may be times when you've hated your adolescent — and still do. You may have even told him so. But it's important to know the difference between hating your child and hating his *behavior*.

Ms. Booker is able to pinpoint the biggest regret she has as a parent: "I had just *had it* with Brandy one day. I couldn't even stand the sight of her, and I told her so. I told her I hated her. In that moment, I really did. I'll never forget the look on her face, and I wish I could take it back."

It's easy to lose sight of the need to love your child, unconditionally. Unconditional love means that, while you might hate the choices your adolescent makes, you still love and accept him for who he is. Your first reaction may be, "I do accept my child, faults and all." But stop and really think about it for a minute. Think about the zingers, emotions and, especially, the expectations.

Accepting your child unconditionally means letting go of past hurts and disappointments caused by unmet expectations. It means still loving your child, who just called you a nasty name, even if you're hurt and angry. If there's ever been a time when you've wondered what's kept you going, unconditional love is probably the answer. It's helped you hang in there.

Unconditional love doesn't mean loving all of Jack's behaviors. You can make it clear to your teen that, although sometimes you hate his behavior, you still love him as only a parent can. There are several ways you can communicate this. First, believe it or not, he needs to hear it – even if his actions scream otherwise. Second, you can make sure you don't withdraw yourself or your love from your child – intentionally or unintentionally.

It can be hard to forgive your child after all the times you've felt hurt, angry, disappointed or rejected. It might seem impossible to get past those feelings and tell him you love him. You may have to fake it at first. Ms. Booker once thought she would never be able to sincerely tell her daughter that she loved her. So she *faked it, until she made it.* In doing so, she was able to go to sleep at night without feeling guilty. She went to bed knowing she hadn't said anything to Brandy that she would regret later. Eventually, she was able to tell Brandy that she loved her — sincerely.

Another benefit of the *fake it until you make it* technique is that it can help both a parent and child feel better. What if something had happened to Brandy, and the last thing Ms. Booker had said to her daughter was, "I hate you"? By faking unconditional love until she actually felt it, Ms. Booker knew that if anything happened, Brandy would know her mother loved her.

Your adolescent still needs your love, no matter what choices he makes. When a parent withholds love, a child knows it – he *feels* it. So do adults, for that matter. Do you have a personal experience with your own parent withdrawing love? Many adults still hurt because their parents don't love and accept them unconditionally. If you haven't had that experience, picture it for a minute. Is there anything you could do that would cause your parent to withdraw love? How would that feel?

Some of the saddest adolescents are those who feel hopeless because they believe their behavior has led to the loss of a parent's love. Do they stop making poor choices because of that? No, but they do become very sad, even depressed. On the other hand, a teenager who knows his parent loves him does *not* necessarily think that same parent loves his negative behaviors. If a stranger asked your adolescent today, "Does your parent love you?" what would he say? Would he be right?

CHAPTER SIXTEEN

School Daze

*T*his chapter is about how to deal with your adolescent's school. This is not a fun topic. Reading this chapter may stir up all sorts of emotions, especially anger. Frankly, writing this chapter got us, the authors, all worked up. That's because we know how terribly frustrating it can be to deal with some school systems. But if you're going to handle the situation in a way that leaves you less frustrated, we have to use the "S" word (school).

Before you begin this chapter, make plans to do something fun or nurturing for yourself afterward. Rent a funny movie, make plans with someone for dinner, read a funny book. Do something fun and light. You deserve it. Now take a deep breath, and let's figure out how to work with schools.

One More Reason to Hate Mondays

It's 11:00 a.m. on a school day. The phone rings. It's Brandy's teacher. She's frustrated because Brandy simply *will not* follow instructions. Ms. Booker thinks to herself sarcastically, *Oh, no, not my kid. She's usually so easy to control.* The teacher continues, "You need to get Brandy's behavior under control. I can't have her disrupting the classroom. You need to come pick her up right now and let her know she isn't to come back until she can behave *appropriately*."

Across town Mrs. Whippet's phone rings. It's the principal. He's calling because Slug hasn't been to school in almost a week. Just what is Mrs. Whippet going to do about the situation, he asks. If she doesn't get her son to school tomorrow, the principal threatens, he'll be forced to call the court and turn her in for educational neglect. After all, she's his mother, which means she's responsible for him getting to school. Mrs. Whippet hangs up the phone, feeling like a kid in trouble herself. *Just what the heck is educational neglect, anyway?* she wonders. *And why am I responsible for making Slug get out of bed?*

In *the old days*, adolescents were often kept home by their parents to help on the farm or to take care of younger children. Parents didn't *have to* let their children attend school. If Jill really wanted to go to school, and she begged and pleaded, her parents could still say, "No." Education was a privilege, not a right.

Eventually society decided *the old way* wasn't acceptable. Laws were passed making it every child's *right* to go to school – whether a parent agreed or not. If Jill wants an education, no one can keep her from going to school. Children became legally obligated to attend some type of school until the age of sixteen (eighteen in some states). If a parent did refuse to allow a child to attend school, that parent could be charged with *educational neglect*.

Educational Neglect

In our country today, *educational neglect* has taken on a whole new meaning. What started out as a way to protect Jill is now used to intimidate and bully parents at times. The same law that protects Jill is used to threaten parents who have kids like Jack. And Jack doesn't *want* to go to school. He may even refuse.

Some parents end up in court because an adolescent won't go to school. Knowing the difference between educational neglect and truancy will help protect you, if you find yourself in that situation. *Educational neglect* occurs when a parent puts no effort into providing a child the opportunity to go to school.

- A family moves to a new district, and the parent never enrolls the child in school.

- A parent has a younger child, and doesn't bother to wake him up or help him get to school.

- A parent isn't around in the morning at all and makes no other arrangements to help a child get to school.

- A child or adolescent is made to stay home and babysit while a parent goes off to work.

Educational neglect is when *a parent fails* to do what he or she can to help their child make it to school.

Truancy

Truancy occurs when an older child or adolescent *refuses* to go to school, no matter what a parent does to encourage him to attend.

- A parent wakes up a teen in the morning, and he refuses to get out of bed.

- An adolescent pretends he's heading to school and instead skips class.

When a child is old enough that he no longer physically needs a parent's help to get to school, and he actually sabotages that parent's efforts, he is truant. If an adolescent is truant, *he* is the one who faces court charges, not the parent.

Refusing to go to school is not a safety issue. However, many parents who are threatened and continually called by the school identify it as a *severe* behavior problem. When Jack refuses to go to school, the big question is, "What can I do as a parent?" By now you know the answer right away: you can stay on your TOES. Go back to Chapter Six (page 55) for an example on how to use the TOES technique when it comes to school. Here are some other things you *can* do:

Communicate With Your Child — See if you can find out *why* your adolescent refuses to go to school. Talk to him. Is he struggling with the work and needs help he isn't getting? That could leave him frustrated, wanting to avoid school. Does he need a tutor? Is he having trouble with peers or a teacher? Ask him to share what's going on in his school life.

Communicate With the School — Talk with your adolescent's teachers and/or principal. Try to listen without taking things personally or getting upset, so you can get the information you need. What goes on during Jack's day? What are his strengths? Are there parts of school he seems to like or does well in? Does the teacher have any ideas about why Jack is avoiding school?

Ask for suggestions — What would the teacher or principal suggest you do? What has the school tried so far to help with your adolescent's school problems? Ask for a copy of the school's rules and policies, and a student handbook.

Investigate Special Education — If your child is in therapy, talk with his therapist about reasons he may be avoiding school. Some kids have trouble interacting appropriately with others, and need to be in a smaller classroom. Talk with the therapist or school social worker about whether or not your child may qualify for special education under *emotional impairment*. Some adolescents also have learning disabilities that have gone unnoticed. This would also mean special education is needed.

If you think your adolescent may need special services, or if you're having a difficult time dealing with school officials, call your Intermediate School District office. Ask how to get a *parent advocate*. An advocate will help you make sure the school is doing *its* part to provide Jack the educational opportunities to which he's entitled. You can also purchase a parent handbook on special education at your local bookstore, or ask for a handbook from the Intermediate School District office. The school is *required by law* to give you information on your rights and your child's rights regarding special education. But it may be a long fight to get your child's rights addressed.

Consider Alternatives — If, after talking with your adolescent and the school, it seems clear he simply doesn't want to go to school, you may consider alternatives. Are there any alternative education programs in your community? Some are provided by both public schools and local colleges. Is home-schooling an option? There are also correspondence schools that will mail materials to your teen for a fee. Would he like that as a Christmas gift? Ask your teen to think honestly about educational alternatives that might be better for him (which doesn't include sitting at home in his boxers watching television all day.)

Some adolescents *go* to school . . . they just get into trouble once they get there. Sleeping in class, refusing to do the work, fighting with peers, threatening or swearing at teachers . . . there's so much for Jack to do in a day. When an adolescent has such problems at school, it's important to remember those are *his* problems. All you can do as a parent is stay on your TOES. If you do that, and your teen continues to make choices that make school difficult, *he* will be the one to experience the consequences. If his choices lead him to fail, be suspended or expelled, those are natural consequences. Remember what happens when you try to protect Jack from natural consequences.

It was hard for Ms. Booker to avoid getting drawn into taking responsibility for Brandy's behavior at school. Lots of people *wanted* her to take on that responsibility: the teacher, principal, her own mother and especially Brandy. She constantly got phone calls from the school that would have been funny if it hadn't been so frustrating. Once, the principal called to tell Ms. Booker that Brandy was refusing to clean up after herself in the lunch room: "She left a bunch of napkins and her tray on the table, and she's refusing to go pick it up." Ms. Booker's response was, "I don't know what to tell you. I have the same problem with her at home. Let me know if you figure out a solution, and I'll try it here."

It took a lot of practice, but eventually Ms. Booker learned to respond to such calls with pocket responses like, "I'm sorry she's having a tough day today. I guess she'll have to experience whatever your consequences are." She also set limits on how often her work and life were disrupted to take care of her daughter's situations: "I won't be able to pick Brandy up early from school today because I have to work. You can have her wait in the office until the time she usually goes home." When she received phone calls of a serious nature, like the time Brandy got into a fist fight with a peer, she responded appropriately by going up to the school in person.

Problems with Jack related to school will be one of two things: he either won't go, or he'll get into trouble once he gets there. In either case, you can control only how you respond to the situation. Ms. Booker couldn't *make* Brandy clean up her mess in the lunch room. Mrs. Whippet couldn't *make* Slug go to school. As a parent, all you can do is stay on your TOES and allow your adolescent to experience the natural consequences of his behavior.

Know Your Areaís Rules

Every child, parent, school and teacher is unique. The experience you have with your adolescent's school will depend on several things, including the state in which you live. Laws and policies differ, and you'll need to contact your Intermediate School District office to find out about your state. Schools can be intimidating. They have a lot of power. They have the public funding and very little competition. They can choose to work with you or against you.

Jack is usually every public school's nightmare. The principal told Top Dog's mother that her son was no longer allowed to attend their school because of his continued tardiness and general negative behaviors. What the principal didn't tell her was that *he had no legal right to give such an order*. He counted on the fact that Top Dog's mother, like many parents, didn't know her son's rights. He was wrong. Top Dog's mother knew that every child has the right to a public education (except in extreme situations). If his behavior meant he could no longer attend, then it was the school's responsibility to provide an alternative.

Top Dog's mom called her Intermediate School District office and moved up the ladder, talking with officials and school board members. She found out that Top Dog could indeed remain at their public school. Then she talked with her son, who told her he didn't *want* to continue at that school. She decided to enroll him in an alternative education program through a community college.

Five months into the program, Top Dog's mother received a phone call from the director. *Oh, no,* she thought. *Here we go again.* She actually cried when the director said he was calling to tell her what a bright, friendly, all-around neat kid she had: "He's a leader, and we're thrilled to have him here." Top Dog's personality clashed with his public school, but was appreciated in a different environment. He finished the year with a 3.8 grade point average.

Dare to Be Different

There's a popular poem that's often used to show how our culture values individuals who "strike out on their own." "The Road Not Taken," by Robert Frost, discusses coming to a fork in the road and choosing the less-traveled path.

Ironically, a copy of "The Road Not Taken" is hanging in many classrooms today. Individuals who take the road less traveled are risk-takers. They are motivated by what they feel will be the right path for them. They care little about society's expectations. Sound familiar? No one takes the road less traveled more than Jack. For better or worse, he makes his own path.

Jack has the kind of personality that is often described as "rebellious." The world needs those "rebels," because they challenge the way things have always been done (the *status quo*). Society typically embraces the *status quo*. Those in power rarely welcome those who challenge the ways of the majority. It doesn't matter if those rebels are adults, adolescents or children.

The Jacks of the world are the ones who become famous. They're the ones who promote social change and growth. Jack doesn't just *tell* *you* how he thinks things should be, he does something about it. People in general don't like that — especially in public schools.

If your child is having problems at school, it's easy for those problems to spill into your home. You're getting phone calls from the school, and that can leave you angry and frustrated. Your adolescent has a lousy day, and it affects his mood for the rest of the night. Consider ways to lessen the effect school has on Jack's life at home. If he acts up at school, and the natural consequence is that he gets suspended, leave it at that. Don't punish him again. That doesn't mean make it *fun* for him to stay home. But don't provide further consequences if he's already received them at school. It will make his whole life seem to revolve around only problems at school.

Wear Jackís Shoes

Put yourself in Jack's shoes for a minute. Imagine you don't get your paperwork (or some other task) done at your job. Not only do you get reprimanded at work, but when you get home you continue to be punished. You're not allowed to use the phone or watch television. Imagine at the end of your work day, your boss hands you two hours worth of work and says, "Finish this by tomorrow — and no, you don't get paid for it."

Imagine you have a boss you can't stand, who doesn't like you either, and you hate the job itself. Every morning when you get up, you dread getting out of bed. But you're not allowed to quit for three years, or you'll be prosecuted and put in jail or on probation. That's what happens to Jack when he doesn't want to go to school and he's under the legal age. When you're feeling angry and frustrated because of Jack's school problems, try to remember he's not feeling too great himself.

If you or your child have a positive relationship with the school, that's terrific. There are *many* teachers and school officials out there who are willing to work with a family to make things better. Unfortunately, as in any profession, there are lots who aren't. If Jack can push *your* emotional buttons, imagine what he can do to a teacher. That teacher may have difficulty looking past his behavior to the strengths we know Jack has.

Many parents we've worked with have shared stories of being belittled, shamed and condescended to by the school system. This chapter is particularly intended to help parents in that situation recognize they are not alone.

Congratulations. You've survived the chapter. It's over. Now go follow through with your plan to have fun tonight. You'll need to, because tomorrow we're going to deal with the court system!

CHAPTER SEVENTEEN

I Left My Sense of Humor on the Courthouse Steps

Mrs. Whippet is getting ready for court. Slug is being charged with truancy — he's been in school only ten days this semester. The principal is following through with his threat. He'll be attending today's hearing so he can tell the judge that Mrs. Whippet should be charged with educational neglect.

As Mrs. Whippet nervously looks through her closet, wondering what clothes will show the judge she is a *good, concerned parent,* a talk show is on the television. She glances at the TV, and on the screen is a boy who reminds her of Slug. The boy slouches in his seat as if nothing in life matters to him; the audience is booing. Today's show is titled, "Kids who need boot camp." The host shakes his head at the boy in exaggerated sadness. The boy's mother is sobbing: "I just don't know what to do with him anymore. He won't listen. I can't control him. He needs to go to boot camp." Mrs. Whippet, already afraid of what will happen in court today, wonders sadly, "Is that the only thing left? Boot camp?"

Ms. Booker is also getting ready for court. Unlike Mrs. Whippet, Ms. B's not worried or scared — she's mad. Court is nothing new for her. She believes she knows exactly what will happen today. Right now, Brandy is on probation for incorrigibility, which basically means refusing to follow her parent's rules. There is a hearing today to determine whether or not she will continue to be on probation, or if her case will be dismissed. In the past month, Brandy has continued to break curfew, swears at her mother constantly, and has snuck out to parties where alcohol and marijuana were the main attraction. Ms. Booker plans on making sure the judge knows *exactly* what her daughter has been doing. She's even made a list of Brandy's negative behaviors, in case the prosecutor needs some help.

As Ms. Booker gets ready, she watches the same talk show the Whippets have on television. A loudmouthed teenage girl with rings in her nose is screaming at the audience, which is screaming back. *There's my kid*, thinks Ms. Booker. "Send her snotty little ass to boot camp," she shouts at the TV, "maybe she'll learn a lesson!" In the back of her mind, Ms. Booker is hoping the judge will place her daughter in a detention or residential center because "at least she won't end up pregnant or catching AIDS if she's locked up."

Top Dog's mother is rifling through *his* closet, trying to find something suitable for him to wear to court today. He was arrested on his second drunk driving offense, along with an assault and battery charge. Last year the judge warned Top Dog that he would send him to jail if he saw him again. Top Dog's mom is sick and terrified, especially because he's scheduled in front of the same judge today. She spent all morning on the phone to the expensive lawyer she hired for her son, trying to figure out a way to get the case moved to a new judge (one who's a little more understanding.) She's taken the entire day off of work, so she can attend the hearing, and, hopefully, help her son.

Top Dog's mother shakes her head sadly at the talk show on television, the one sending teenagers to boot camp. She pictures Top Dog in such a place, and it makes her so sick she turns the TV off. She pulls out the suit she bought Top Dog for last year's Homecoming dance (the one she had dry-cleaned after he threw-up on it in a drunken stupor). She looks over at her son, who is still in bed. She lays the suit out for him, worrying about what will happen today.

When It Comes to Court

Sometimes an adolescent's behavior results in the court becoming involved. Repeatedly breaking curfew, destroying property, incorrigibility, running away, substance use or possession, assault and theft are all acts that may lead to charges being filed. When that happens, whipped parents react in different ways.

Some parents, like Ms. Booker, have simply "had it" with their adolescent. They're ready to try anything, send their child anywhere, in the hope that it will "straighten him out." Teachers, therapists, friends, family and especially some of today's talk show hosts are full of suggestions: foster care, detention centers, military school and the ever-popular boot camps.

The glitch in those answers is that *kids aren't disposable.* There is no return or exchange policy. And the reality is, there simply is no place to put a generation of Jacks, who don't or won't meet society's expectations. Believe it or not, that's not a *bad* thing. Sending an adolescent "away" because he isn't meeting the expectations of parents or society should *not* be a quick or easy option. Your child may make choices that result in the natural consequence of court involvement. In extreme cases, the court may take custody and send that child to some type of placement. That's *very* different from a parent threatening to send that child away because of his behavior.

Threatening your adolescent with foster care or boot camp is not only unrealistic, it usually makes the situation worse. First, those placements are typically court-ordered, and judges see that option as a last resort (unless you are on a talk show). The court's goal is to keep families together. Foster care or boot camp are used only after many other things have been tried. They are also *very* expensive, and parents are ordered to pay as much of that bill as possible. Voluntary foster care placements are rare because of the tremendous financial burden on parents. Besides, how realistic is it to place your child in foster care until he's eighteen years old? How long can the average parent afford to pay up to $200 a day for foster care? Military schools are also expensive, sometimes as much as $20,000 for a year, and they are voluntary. That means your child must *want* to go.

Before you threaten your adolescent with any of these options, make sure you understand that you will probably be unable to follow through with that threat. If you are, you need to be aware that these options are rarely successful on a long-term basis. When a child first returns from such a placement, he may try harder to behave as you'd like. Eventually, however, he will probably act out even more. Jack is already fighting against being controlled. In the long run, how do you think he will react to his parent sending him to a place that physically forces control on him?

The Truth About Placement

Military schools and boot camps are based on the approach of breaking a child's spirit and personality, then trying to build it back up the way others would like it to be. Be well-informed about what goes on in these places. Adolescents we work with have returned with stories of being ridiculed, screamed at, forced to stand naked in a small holding cell for up to twenty-four hours at a time. They are often forced to run long distances, whether they are physically capable of doing so or not. Kids have reported being struck physically by those who run such places. Before you attempt to send your adolescent, ask yourself if you would be prepared to have *your own* spirit and personality broken. Could you endure what some of these adolescents go through? How would you feel if your own parent was the one who sent you there?

Not all parents are prepared for their child to be sent away. Some, like Top Dog's mother, want to rescue their adolescent from the court system. It's important to remember that probation and detention centers are natural consequences to some illegal behaviors. If an adolescent chooses to engage in such behaviors, he *must* be allowed to experience those consequences. No matter how badly a parent may feel for him. Rescuing your adolescent will only make the situation worse.

Finally, some parents (like Mrs. Whippet) are frightened when their child becomes involved with the court. What will happen to him? Can *I* get in trouble for anything he's done? How much of my child's behavior is the judge going to hold *me* responsible for?

In general, police, judges, lawyers and probation officers want to work *with* you and your child. Their goal is for your adolescent to remain in your home, and the court will attempt any intervention it can to avoid placement outside the home. The court and police may be a resource to you when you feel that, despite staying on your TOES, your adolescent continues to engage in behaviors that threaten you or your family. Examples are when your child assaults you, destroys your property, steals from you or runs away. In those situations, you will need the help of community agencies:

The Police

When your adolescent is behaving illegally, you will need the help or advice of the police. The first step is to pay a visit to the station at a time when you are feeling emotionally calm and stable. Ask to speak with an officer about your adolescent's behavior. If you've already had contact with the police and know a particular officer you feel might be helpful, ask for him or her. Let him know what's been going on in your home, and tell the officer what you've done to stay on your TOES. Ask for suggestions on how to handle things the next time your adolescent engages in behaviors that are legal or safety issues.

Many parents feel that police, in general, are not helpful with their adolescent. Remember, some police officers are just as frustrated with today's adolescents as parents may be. You may encounter an officer who makes inappropriate suggestions, such as "Beat his ass." In that case, simply pursue suggestions from a different officer, one who may be more willing to approach the situation realistically (and in a way that won't backfire and get *you* in trouble). Some officers become frustrated when they are called repeatedly to a home for non-safety situations (like a teenager being generally belligerent). However, if you can show the police that you are genuinely interested in the best way to handle safety situations, they will be more likely to work with you. As a team, you can develop a plan for how you will respond to future situations.

Remember not to sabotage your teen once that plan has been developed. Donít set him up. Use the plan only as a safety net, a last resort.

The Court as a Resource

The court may be helpful when you have exhausted alternatives to dealing with your adolescent's behavior. If your adolescent repeatedly refuses to follow most or all of your house rules, even though you've stayed on your TOES, you may contact the court about charging him with incorrigibility. Keep in mind though, if you choose to pursue the matter through the court, you *will* end up with some significant legal costs. Speak with someone at the court about what you can expect to pay, so you can make an informed decision.

If it's necessary for you to call the police because your child destroys your property or assaults you, make sure you follow through with the court system.

Donít just drop the matter by dropping the charges.

Your teen may end up on probation or in detention because of his actions. This may or may not fall on you financially. He may push your guilt button for having followed through with the court. *Donít dance with him.* It's important for him to experience those natural consequences.

If your adolescent does end up on probation (for any reason), following a few basic guidelines will help you stay on your TOES. First, try to remember that the probation officer is not your enemy. He or she is involved with your family *because of choices your adolescent has made.* Second, remember to stay on middle ground. Keep in contact with your child's probation officer as needed, but don't call (or threaten to call) for every little thing. Stay away from the extreme of sabotaging your child. On the other hand, don't lie for your adolescent. Rescuing him from natural consequences will backfire. Try to let your adolescent deal with the conditions of his probation on his own as much as possible. After all, it was *his* choices that got him into this situation.

The court, in particular your child's probation officer if he has one, should also be able to tell you about other resources in your community. These may include runaway shelters or programs, counseling services, mentors and family reunification programs.

Other Resources

Each community has different programs and resources for families. Some agencies are funded by the federal government and should be available in all states. These include local Community Mental Health agencies (CMH). CMH organizations offer a wide range of services, including therapy for you and/or your adolescent, home-based programs, and respite services. Look in your local phone book for The United Way, or an agency similar to it, that can provide you with a list of specific resources in your community.

Stop

Old habits are hard to break. Changing the way you think and react to your child may be the most difficult challenge you'll face as a parent. Mrs. Whippet, Ms. Booker and Top Dog's mother all fell into old habits while preparing for court. Remembering what they had learned, each of these parents realized they were slipping into "old" ways of thinking and acting.

Rewind . . .

Mrs. Whippet stopped frantically looking through her closet. Because she had learned the difference between educational neglect and truancy, she was prepared when she went to court with Slug. Mrs. Whippet told the judge about efforts she's made to help Slug get up in the morning and how she's tried to stay on her TOES. She took along the calendar she had used to keep track of school personnel with whom she'd spoken. She let her son explain *his own* actions, hopeful that he would be prepared to accept the consequences of those choices. Mrs. Whippet was not charged with educational neglect. Slug was placed on probation for truancy and assigned a truancy officer.

Ms. Booker stopped shouting at the talk show on television. She calmed down enough to realize that she was at an emotional extreme: sabotaging. She attended court with Brandy but didn't give a written list of her daughter's behavior to the prosecutor. When the judge asked her questions, Ms. Booker answered them honestly, without trying to sway the court into sending Brandy away. Brandy's probation was extended. Ms. Booker stayed on middle ground and left the hearing feeling good about herself as a parent.

Top Dog's mother worked hard at controlling her feelings, which silently screamed: *rescue your son . . . at all costs.* She called a friend from Al-Anon before going to her son's court hearing. She realized she was at the emotional extreme of rescuing her child. She put the suit back in the closet, leaving the decision of what Top Dog would wear up to him. She calmly told herself she would not hire any more lawyers or miss any more work due to her son's behavior. She allowed Top Dog to experience the natural consequences of his actions without trying to convince the court otherwise. Although the thought of Top Dog going to jail still made her sick to her stomach, she reminded herself that the thought of jail must not bother Top Dog as much as it bothered her. If it did, he would stop pushing the limits of society. Top Dog's mom continued to take steps to keep *herself* healthy.

Keeping Yourself Healthy

Trying to maintain a healthy stance in life while continuing to parent a difficult teen is a challenging task. Up to this point, we have asked you to do a lot of tough things. Now we are going to ask you to give yourself a break. One of the nicest gifts you can give yourself is nurturance. The next chapter will help you get started.

CHAPTER EIGHTEEN

Nurturing Yourself

*Y*ou weren't always a whipped parent. Once upon a time, you had a life. Think back . . . Some of you may have to think back farther than others. Are there things that you've given up since problems started with Jack? Friends, hobbies, time for yourself? Being whipped leaves little or no time for *fun*.

Balancing Your Life

This is the last chapter. By now, you know you can't control your adolescent. The flip side of that coin is that he can't control you, either. He can't — no matter how hard he tries, unless you let him. You have control over how you choose to spend your life.

It's so easy to get caught up in your role as a parent that you forget to nurture other parts of your life. Think about all the different roles you've had during your life: spouse or lover, friend, employee or supervisor, daughter or son, sister or brother. You may fall into the trap of thinking, "Well, I just can't take any time for myself. I'm too busy taking care of things with Jack." Your life may be focused on, or even consumed with, your adolescent.

If you find yourself so wrapped up in your adolescent that you don't take care of *yourself* anymore – that's a problem. You're no good to your child if you're so whipped you don't have the time or energy to find anything enjoyable in life. If you want to stay on your TOES, you have to *show* him that life can be full and balanced.

If you feel like you've been able to hang onto those parts of your life that give you joy, great. It's a hard thing to do, even with a child like Jill (let alone Jack). In our society, being a parent is considered one of (if not *the*) most important roles you can have. Unfortunately, that belief can turn unhealthy, even dangerous, if you don't balance that role with other things. It's about finding middle ground: your child should be important, but not all-consuming. Have you ever known anyone who can't seem to find *anything* to talk about — except their child? We all fall into that trap sometimes. When it becomes a long-standing pattern, it's time to make some changes.

Believe it or not, most kids don't want to be responsible for your happiness. It scares them. They may eventually push against you even harder to send the message, "Hey, don't make *me* the center of your life." Even if a child's behavior shouts, *I want all of your attention, all of the time*, in the end he will resent being that focus. On the surface, Jack may make it hard for you to find time to focus on other things. In the long run, he'll respect you more for doing so.

Top Dog's mom wasn't the only one who worried in their home. Top Dog worried, too — about his mom. He was the focus of her time, energy and thoughts. She lost touch with family and friends in her efforts to help or change her son. How would she survive if something happened to him or he wasn't around? Top Dog believed if he was ever in an accident or even moved to another state, his mother would fall apart. It wasn't a good feeling. In fact, it made him scared, angry and resentful.

The parents in this book found middle ground by taking their kids' advice. Each of them decided to "get a life." Mrs. Whippet rejoined a card club she belonged to before Slug became a teenager. She and Mr. Whippet started going out to dinner every Saturday night – alone. They agreed not to mention Slug's name on those nights out. Ms. Booker started bowling again, something she had once enjoyed a lot. She even took a chance and started dating again. Top Dog's mom started attending Al-Anon meetings every week and got in touch again with friends she'd lost. She goes to a massage therapist once a month.

The key to finding middle ground is balance. There are bound to be times when things get put on the back burner because of a situation with your adolescent. But it's important to reel things back in by taking care of yourself as well. Make a list of things you can do to nurture yourself. Then make a commitment to yourself to follow through and *do them*. If such a thought is too tiring or overwhelming to you, think seriously about seeing a counselor or therapist. You may be depressed, and that's understandable. The important thing is that you start taking care of yourself, even if you need some help doing that.

After all, you deserve it!

The Journey

by Rodney Studaker

I think I see, it's dawning on me,
I'm able to break from this trap.
It's time for fun, I'm finally done,
I refuse to wallow in CRAP.

No ups or downs, I'll seek middle ground,
I'll keep my life under control.
I will survive, I may even thrive,
If I can remember to stay on my TOES.

When Jack (or Jill) make me want to kill,
I simply won't join in the game.
I won't fall prey to what others say,
I'll refuse to take all the blame.

Now I will deal with the way that I feel,
I'll keep expectations in line.
My hopes run wild, for my challenging child,
But those dreams are not his — they're mine.

I took a look at this helpful book,
And one thing I now clearly see:
We will get by, my child and I,
But first I must take care of me.

The Road Ahead...

You've reached the end of your journey with us, but your journey with your child continues for a lifetime. It is a lifelong process. The techniques and ideas in this book can help get you started toward the emotional growth and well-being you will need to sustain you as you travel down the road of life with your adolescent. As your child reaches adulthood, he may continue to challenge your personal growth. You may continue to find yourself "along for the ride" on paths he chooses to take (even when he's thirty years old). If you still feel he's an awful driver, you may choose not to go along for those rides.

Emotional well-being doesn't happen overnight. It takes commitment, patience and the acceptance that you may slip along the way. You may even take some hard falls. The key is to pick yourself back up, brush yourself off and regain your balance. Strive ahead, and don't give up.

Reading this book has given you a set of tools you can use in the journey with your child. However, becoming skilled at using those tools will take practice and much effort. Remember, old habits can be *very* hard to break, and it's human nature to slide back into those old ways of thinking and acting. That's why we call them *parent traps*. The more you stick with the approach in this book, the sooner it will become part of your daily life ... your *new* habit. You may need to go back and read certain chapters again ... and again. The more you keep refreshing yourself, the better you'll feel. We wish you luck and happiness with your continued journey.

The Serenity Prayer

God, grant me the serenity to accept the things I cannot change
The courage to change the things that I can
And the wisdom to know the difference

Appendix A
Staying on Your TOES

The first TOES worksheet is about your *Hopes*, the second about your *Expectations*. Remember, there's a big difference between hopes and expectations: a hope is something you *wish for* for your child, while an expectation is something *you count on* to happen. When you start feeling frustrated, guilty or angry because your teen isn't meeting a hope or expectation, use one of these worksheets to make certain you've done all that *you* can do to provide opportunities for your child. Go back to Chapter Six (page 53), if you need an example of how to use the worksheets, to remind yourself that you've done all that you *can* do as a parent. The rest is up to your adolescent! If there's one expectation or hope you're having a particularly hard time with, make a note card to hang on your refrigerator. It will remind you how to stay on your TOES about that issue.

Staying On Your TOES

Example One: HOPES

State the problem: _____

_____

_____

Tell him _____.

Opportunities presented to help him meet my hope:

- I *can* _____
- I *can* _____
- I *can* _____
- I *can* _____
- I *can* _____
- I *can* _____

Educate him with knowledge to help him choose whether or not he's going to try to meet my hope:

- I *can* _____
- I *can* _____
- I *can* _____
- I *can* _____
- I *can* _____

Show (or model) it.

- I *can* _____
- I *can* _____
- I *can* _____
- I *can* _____

Staying On Your TOES

Example Two: EXPECTATIONS

State the problem: _____
_____
_____

Tell him _____.

Opportunities presented to help him meet my expectation:

- I *can* _____
- I *can* _____
- I *can* _____
- I *can* _____
- I *can* _____
- I *can* _____

Educate him with knowledge to help him choose whether or not he's going to try to meet my expectation:

- I *can* _____
- I *can* _____
- I *can* _____
- I *can* _____
- I *can* _____

Show (or model) it.

- I *can* _____
- I *can* _____
- I *can* _____
- I *can* _____

Appendix B
The Thunderstorm
Worksheet

This worksheet will help you change your actions and feelings by changing your thoughts. At first, you'll work your way *down* the worksheet. Start by picking a negative action of your own that you're unhappy about, such as yelling at your child. Then skip down to the negative feelings and identify what you were feeling just before that action occurred. Remember, this takes some effort and probably some practice, as well. After you've pinpointed the feelings you were experiencing, continue on to identify the thoughts you had that led to those negative emotions. Finally, begin working your way back *up* the worksheet by identifying positive replacement thoughts for the previously negative ones. Move up to list the new feelings that will come from these new thoughts, and, finally, to the new actions others will see. Refer back to Chapter Nine (page 73) for an example of how to use The Thunderstorm model.

The Thunderstorm Worksheet

Negative Actions _____

_____

New Actions: _____

_____

Negative Feelings _____

_____

New Feelings: _____

_____

Negative Thoughts

Thought _____

(replacement thought_____)

Thought _____

(replacement thought_____)

Thought _____

(replacement thought_____)

Thought _____

(replacement thought_____)

Appendix C
The Control List

Using the worksheet on the following page will help you identify fail-proof consequences that are based on things you can truly control. The first step in developing fail-proof consequences for your adolescent is to identify things over which you have complete control. Some examples include giving your teen rides to places and events, buying expensive clothing or fast food for him, money spent on birthdays and holidays, magazine subscriptions, or allowing your teen to use your car. Examples of things over which you do *not* have complete control include grounding (he can sneak out or just plain leave), taking away his things (he can break into your room and get them), and giving extra chores (you can't physically force him to follow through and do them). After you've completed The Control List, you can remove identified "extras" in response to your teen's negative behaviors (see Appendix D, page 159, for more on developing fail-proof consequences). The important thing is to make sure that you have complete control over what you've identified.

The Control List

Things you do for your adolescent that are a privilege, not a right. List all the extras and things over which you have complete control.

_____

_____

_____

_____

_____

_____

_____

_____

_____

_____

_____

_____

_____

_____

_____

_____

_____

_____

_____

_____

Appendix D
Fail-proof Consequences
Worksheet

This worksheet will help you develop fail-proof consequences to use in response to your adolescent's negative behavior. Remember, with a child like Jack, you may be limited to a few fail-proof consequences, so use them only when necessary, and be consistent.

In the first column, start by selecting a consequence you think may be fail-proof. Be specific. What is the length of time for which the consequence will be given? When will it start and end? Next, in column two, check to see if the consequence is really fail-proof. List all of the possible reactions your teen may have to this consequence — everything you can think of. Then, use column three to decide if you still have complete control over the consequence.

If you're thinking of grounding your child, and one of the possible reactions is that he might sneak out a window and leave anyway, you do not have complete control — your adolescent does. Using a consequence over which you do not have complete control will backfire and leave you feeling more angry, frustrated and powerless. On the other hand, if you decide not to give your child a ride somewhere the next time he wants one, you do have complete control over the situation. Even if your teen steals a car or hitchhikes, you still didn't give him a ride. Finally, in the last column, evaluate whether or not you can live through your teen's reactions. If not, you might end up suffering more than he does, and your consequence will probably fail. However, don't refrain from using consequences because he might react in a way that's illegal or causes negative natural consequences for himself — that's his choice.

Your child may say that he doesn't care about the consequence you develop. That's okay. Kids often say, "I don't care," or "So what?" In reality, some do care and just aren't going to let you know it. Also, it doesn't matter if he cares or not. The important thing is that you are showing him that there are consequences to the choices he makes.

Fail-proof Consequences Worksheet

STEP ONE	STEP TWO	STEP THREE	STEP FOUR
Develop a consequence that I think may be fail-proof.	List all possible ways he may respond to this consequence.	Review each response to learn if I still have control.	Evaluate his reactions. Can you live through them?

The publisher grants photocopy and enlargement rights to the reader for personal use only.

Suggested Reading

Are You in Control: A Handbook For Those Who Want to Be in Control of Their Lives by Wendy Grant. ISBN 1-85230-778-1

Chicken Soup for the Soul: Cartoons for Moms by Jack Canfield, Mark Victor Hansen and John McPherson. ISBN 0-7573-0087-1

The Co-Dependent Parent: Free Yourself by Freeing Your Child by Barbara Cottman Becnel. ISBN 0-06-250126-7

Courage to Change: One Day at a Time in Al-Anon II by Al-Anon Family Groups *for families and friends of alcoholics.* ISBN 0-910034-79-6

Divorce Poison by Dr. Richard A. Warshak. ISBN 0-06-018899-5

The Essential Guide to the New Adolescent: How to Raise an Emotionally Healthy Teenager by Ava L. Siegler, Ph.D. ISBN 0-525-93970-9

I Donít Have To Make Everything All Better: A Practical Approach to Walking Emotionally With Those You Care About While Empowering Them to Solve Their Own Problems by Gary B. Lundberg and Joy Saunders Lundberg. ISBN 0-915029-02-2

Meditations for Women Who Do Too Much by Anne Wilson Schaef. ISBN 0-06-251437-7

Natural Mental Health: How to Take Control of Your Own Emotional Well-being by Carla Wills-Brandon, Ph.D. ISBN 1-56170-727-9

One Day At A Time In Al-Anon. ISBN 0-910034-21-4

Parents Who Love Too Much by Cheryl Irwin and Jane Nelson. ISBN 0-76152-142-9

Parents With Broken Hearts by William L. Coleman. ISBN 0-8007-8692-0

Pleasant Dreams: Nighttime Meditations for Peace of Mind by Amy E. Dean. ISBN 1-56170-693-0

Pulling Your Own Strings: Dynamic techniques for dealing with other people and living your life as you choose by Wayne W. Dyer. ISBN 0-06-091975-2

Self Esteem, 3rd Edition by Matthew McKay, Ph.D., and Patrick Fanning. ISBN 1-57224-198-5

The Self Esteem Companion by Matthew McKay, Ph.D., Patrick Fanning, Carol Honeychurch and Catharine Sutker. ISBN 1-57224-138-1

Thereís a Spiritual Solution to Every Problem by Wayne W. Dyer. ISBN 0-06-019230-5

You Canít Afford The Luxury Of A Negative Thought: A Book for People With Any Life-Threatening Illness ó Including Life by John-Roger and Peter McWilliams. ISBN 0-931580-20-X

Index

Index   173

About the Authors

Kimberly Abraham began her career as an Early Childhood educator, working with children and families in the Flint, Michigan-area schools. She went on to receive her Master of Social Work Degree from Wayne State University, with a concentration in Family, Youth & Children. She has been certified as an Infant Mental Health Specialist and provided social work services to children in Flint-area schools. Kim has spent years providing services to youth in the city of Flint, Michigan, working closely with systems such as REACH, Flint Schools and the Genesee Circuit Family Court. She specializes in treating children & adolescents diagnosed with Oppositional Defiant Disorder (ODD), Conduct Disorder and Substance Abuse.

In 2003, Kim co-authored *The Whipped Parent: Hope for Parents Raising an Out-of-Control Teen* (Rainbow Books, Inc) with her colleague and business partner, Marney Studaker-Cordner, LMSW. The book is based on Kim's personal experience raising an ODD son, as well as professional knowledge and techniques field-tested with parents individually and in group settings. In 2011, Kim and Marney went on to create *Life Over The Influence* (Legacy Publishing Company), a CD self-help program for those who love someone who has an addiction or abuses substances. *The Oppositional Defiant Disorder Lifeline* (Legacy Publishing Company), released in January 2012, is a self-help program for parents of behavior-disordered children based on Kim's unique, specialized parenting approach for that population.

Kim is a national speaker on the topics of childhood behavior disorders and is frequently a media consultant on topics including: bullying, divorce issues, trauma, surviving a loved one's addiction, grandparents raising grandchildren and the increasing epidemic of adult children living at home (Failure to Launch).

Marney Studaker-Cordner, LMSW, received her Master of Social Work from Michigan State University in 1997 with a specialty in Children and Families. She has spent most of her career serving children and families in the Child Welfare and Community Mental Health systems. She is trained in the evidence-based practice of Integrated Dual Disorder Treatment (IDDT) and has supervisory experience in the CMH system. Marney specializes in the treatment of children with emotional and behavioral issues and adults experiencing co-occurring mental health and substance abuse issues. Marney is the parent of a biological daughter and has both professional and personal experience in blended families, having raised three step-children through adolescence and into adulthood.

Kathryn OíDea was an author and ordained minister who passed away in 2006. Kathryn's organizational skills and support were instrumental in the publication of *The Whipped Parent*. She is dearly missed.

Kim and Marney offer a variety of resources, information and materials for parents and professionals through their website, TherapiesInAPod.com. They are available for seminars, coaching and consultation.